CONTENTS

Introduction by Eugene Schwartz v

I. A New Picture of the Human Being 1

II. The Six-Year-Olds 15

III. The Seven-Year-Olds 41

IV. The Eight-Year-Olds 50

V. The Nine-Year-Olds............................. 61

VI. The Ten-Year-Olds 73

VII. The Eleven-Year-Olds 85

VIII. The Twelve-Year-Olds 99

IX. The Thirteen-Year-Olds 109

X. The Temperaments 116

XI. The Teacher 125

XII. Teacher and Child 129

Bibliography 138

iii

INTRODUCTION

Never before has so much been known about child development and educational methodology; yet never before has there been such widespread dissatisfaction with the role of the schools in our society.

Research and development on the university level make education an increasingly "scientific" subject, while an ever-growing number of court cases and legislative measures involving schools and their students makes education a concern of the law as well. Yet what has really been achieved?

The scientific approach to education creates a situation in which both teacher and student meet one another in the cold, clinical guise of "experimenter" and "experimental subject." Pedagogical tests are carried out, wherein more often than not children interact with a machine or computer printout rather than with a human being. Parameters are established, results are compiled, new questions arise leading to the need for new parameters, and the process begins all over again. The sparks of soul and spirit that once passed between teacher and pupil, the enthusiasm, the laughter and joy that could fill a classroom are dismissed as factors too subjective, and hence unscientific, to be quantitatively measured and understood.

The subjugation of our educational institutions by the legislatures and courts creates yet another untenable situation. As the spectre of "student rights" assumes more importance than the quality of the education those students are receiving, the relationship of teacher and student becomes one of defendant and plaintiff. The right of the teacher to innovate, to act out of a sense of personal integrity, or to maintain a loving, healthy discipline in the classroom is undermined, while the child's need to respect rightful authority is sacrificed to an adversarial relationship.

It becomes clear that science and legalism tend to interfere with the educational process rather than enhance it, and that neither widespread experimentation nor well-meaning legislation will be the foundation of future learning. Where, then, *does* education belong? As the title of this book indicates, the renewal of education will arise only inasmuch as education becomes an art. Not, indeed, a solitary artistic mode, but a *lively* art which weaves among the other arts, recombining them and reforming them for the sake of the developing child.

Let us envision the teacher as engaged neither in scientific research nor in litigation, but rather in an artistic activity such as sculpture. The teacher brings to his or her work an ideal vision of the form to be brought from the conceptual sphere into the physical world, and approaches the class with confidence born of training and experience. The stone upon which the teacher will work has *its* own laws as well: it is hard, brittle, and resistant. The sculptor's task is neither to stubbornly assert the primacy of his or her own vision over the stone, nor merely to leave the stone to its own untransformed nature. In the artist's work there must be a *meeting*; in the artistic deed, the artist is in a middle realm, moving between intention and action, subject and object, spirit and matter. The teacher's task is, of course, even more demanding because the nature of the child is rather more complex than that of the stone! Rather than impose a vision, the teacher must perceive what dwells as potential within each child and help it unfold harmoniously.

Marjorie Spock has carefully structured her book not along the lines of abstract subject headings, but rather in accordance with the ages and stages of growth of the child. As a trained artist, she brings enthusiasm and beauty to all that she teaches, but as an experienced farmer she knows that "the ripeness is all." Nothing can be taught to a child until the child is ready to receive it, unless knowledge and vision are to sprout prematurely and wither early.

* * * * *

In her account of the first Waldorf School in Stuttgart, Germany, Marjorie Spock takes us up to the time of its closing by the Nazis in 1938. At the end of the Second World War, the Waldorf School's excellent reputation and uncompromising independence from all political pressures led it to be the first German school re-opened by the American occupation forces. In the post-war years Waldorf schools were founded in virtually every major German city and suburb. At the time of this writing (1985) there are seventy-five such schools in Germany educating over 32,000 students. Research funded by the Bonn Department of Education revealed that, even in conventional terms, Waldorf graduates had achieved "an educational niveau well above the average" and that the artistic approach of the Waldorf pedagogy produced students who are "thoroughly capable in life" (*Der Spiegel*, Dec. 14, 1981).

Waldorf schools have subsequently been founded throughout Europe, in the Western Hemisphere, Australia, New Zealand, South Africa, and India, while growing interest in Japan will soon lead to the first Waldorf school in eastern Asia. Among independent school movements only the Catholic Church sponsors more schools worldwide.

In the seven years that have passed since the 1978 first edition of this book, the number of Waldorf schools in North America has more than doubled, so that now over eighty schools are working with the ideas and methods described in *Teaching as a Lively Art*. Many of these schools are still at the Nursery-Kindergarten stage, beginning the long path of organic growth that leads up through the grades. Eleven schools in the United States include classes from Nursery-Kindergarten through Twelfth Grade. Independent of state aid, the American Waldorf schools foster an environment where the artistry of the teacher and the eagerness and joy of the students can meet and engage in the art of education.

Eugene Schwartz
Green Meadow Waldorf School
Spring Valley, New York
February 1985

The journal *Child and Man* provides insights into the activities and strivings of Waldorf schools in North America and Britain. For information and subscriptions, write to:
    The secretary, *Child and Man,* The Sprig, Ashdown Road, Forest Row, East Sussex, RH19 5BR United Kingdom.

Information about the location and age range of American Waldorf schools can be obtained from:
    Association of Waldorf Schools in North America, David Alsop, 3750 Bannister Road, Fair Oaks, CA 95628.

CHAPTER I

A New Picture of the Human Being

From time to time men of exceptional stature have made their appearance on the stage of history—men who have stood head and shoulders above their contemporaries. There have been poets, philosophers, painters, musicians, playwrights, sculptors, historians and scientists among them. Yet all have had one interest in common: each in his way has sought to throw light on man's being.

The task they faced has been the most exacting one imaginable, for man is a being of immense potentialities. Moreover, he is continually growing. So swift, so transforming is this growth that the artists no sooner touch brush to canvas than the expression on their subject's face changes.

In spite of its difficulties the task has been of such absorbing interest that great men of every period have given their lives to gaining an altitude from which they might view man in all the essential grandeur of his being. The Greek philosophers, Cicero, Leonardo da Vinci, Shakespeare, Goethe, Pascal, Novalis, Emerson, Walt Whitman, Solovieff, have been some of those artist-thinkers who found it natural to seek a comprehensive picture of the human being.

In our own time Rudolf Steiner has joined their company. He has been little known to his contemporaries in the western world. Yet the universality of his genius and the quality of his

1

contributions to human progress predestine him to recognition as one of the great benefactors of mankind.

Rudolf Steiner was born in a little village on the Hungarian-Croatian border in 1861. Even in early childhood he gave evidence of the remarkable endowments he possessed. His was a nature as rich in warmth and sympathy as it was prodigious in intellect. The lively interest he took in every experience, the profound delight he felt in the activity of thinking, led to a precocious ripening of insight and intelligence in this otherwise childlike little schoolboy. He tells in his autobiography how he was fascinated by any book with a philosophical title, how he hung on the words of adults who could speak to him of literature and history and answer his many questions about the world and its riddles. At eight he discovered a geometry textbook on his teacher's desk and plunged with delight into this absorbing subject.

When he was fourteen, he began to tutor young and old alike in whatever subject they desired to learn. If it were new to him, he managed to learn it a few steps ahead of his pupils. In this way he mastered many subjects of a practical as well as academic nature, which became factors in his unusually broad development. From his fourteenth to his thirtieth year he was able to support himself entirely by tutoring while carrying on extensive study and research in almost every field of learning.

As a young man of twenty-one Steiner was engaged as tutor in a family of four children. The youngest, a boy of eleven, was a hydrocephalic child of gravely retarded mental growth and fragile health. Even the slightest effort produced alarming symptoms of fatigue. It seemed doubtful that he could ever be educated. Steiner tells of the extreme care he had to take in his work with the boy. He often spent two hours preparing for a half-hour period of instruction in order that a maximum of learning might be achieved with a minimum of strain. He succeeded so remarkably that after a year and a half of such tutoring the child was able to enter high school. His head grew smaller. In time he was completely restored to health and was able to enter the medical profession, in which he rendered distinguished service. Steiner felt profoundly grateful for having had to teach under these unusual conditions, for it enabled him to gain a deep insight into the learning process—an insight upon which the educational practices described below are based.

During his years of academic study in Vienna, Steiner became keenly interested in the physical sciences. But he rejected the mechanistic view of man and nature held by most contemporary scientists, declaring it to be the product of a basic misconception of scientific method when applied to kingdoms other than the mineral. In his *Theory of Knowledge Implicit in Goethe's World Conception*, published in his twenty-fifth year, he presented a brilliant sketch of the differing scientific methods applicable to the mineral, vegetable, animal and human kingdoms.

When only twenty-two, Steiner was commissioned to edit the scientific writings of Goethe for Kurschner's National Edition of the poet's works. Here was an artist-thinker who aroused his whole enthusiasm. For the next fourteen years he devoted himself to annotating this great man's scientific work. At thirty he was called to the Goethe Archives at Weimar, where he spent seven years collaborating with some of the finest scholars of his day in editing Goethe's still unpublished works. His association with them proved highly stimulating to the development of his own conception of the human being, which he expressed in the widely read *Philosophy of Freedom*.

In the years immediately following Steiner continued to build on this foundation, carrying the basic conception of the free human spirit into every department of learning. A dazzling array of books, articles and lectures on a great variety of subjects bears witness to the extraordinary scope of his knowledge

3

and ability. It enabled him to make contributions not only to philosophy and education but to the arts, history, medicine, physics and agriculture.

Having faithfully labored to master the learning of his time, Steiner proceeded to add significantly to it. Chief among his contributions was the working out of a new science of the human being. Its application to education led to the founding of the Waldorf School at Stuttgart in 1919.

For some time readers and students of Steiner had been anxious to put his educational ideas into practice. This opportunity came through the owner of the Waldorf Cigarette Factory, who proposed establishing a school for the children of his employees. Steiner was asked to organize and direct it.

The school began with 175 boys and girls of all ages and a staff of teachers, chosen not so much for their learning as for their eagerness to learn. Scarcely one among them had ever taught before. Steiner proceeded to give them an intensive training for the special work they were undertaking. To the end of his life he kept in close touch with them. Although he lived in Switzerland and was engaged in important tasks that required his presence there, he made weekly trips to visit the school, giving demonstration lessons and consulting with the faculty on their many problems.

Interest in the new school grew rapidly and soon spread to other countries. Teachers and pupils from all over the world came to study there. In reply to requests for lectures on the methods of the Waldorf School Dr. Steiner traveled through Europe illuminating his basic principles of teaching from ever new aspects. In 1922 he was invited to speak at the International Conference on Spiritual Values in Education held at Oxford University. His ideas awakened great interest there, and he visited England again the following year to give further courses of lectures on educational subjects.

At the time of Steiner's death in 1925 the Waldorf School had

4

grown to seven times its original size. It had become the largest private school on the continent. Other schools of the same pattern were springing up in Europe, England and America.

Hitler's Germany could not long tolerate within its borders this education dedicated to the cultivation of human freedom. The closing of the Waldorf School by the Nazi government in 1938 temporarily ended a great school's career, but it could not blot out the perspectives that had been opened during its nineteen years of life. After the war the school began again, and the Waldorf movement expanded rapidly.

Although Rudolf Steiner had devoted himself for so many years to the task of acquiring a thorough-going knowledge of the thought of his day, though he had refrained from bringing forward his own ideas until this task was accomplished, he was not overawed by contemporary opinion when his keen thinking found it to be in error. His own observations led him to form independent conclusions about the nature of the human being. It was on these conclusions that the educational practices of the Waldorf School were based.

It was obvious to Steiner that human beings were something more than accidental products of a soul-less, mechanically functioning cosmos. He saw in them human spirits, sharing the life and evolution of an essentially spiritual universe—a universe out of which the world of matter had evolved. This material world, he held, everywhere revealed its spiritual origin to those who looked sharply enough to be able to discern it. Nor was he alone in this conviction; many great scientists had come to similar conclusions. Among them was Sir James Jeans whose research caused him to declare in his book, *The Mysterious Universe*, that the universe appeared rather like a great thought than a great machine.

Steiner was not influenced in his observations of the spiritual nature of the universe by any tendency to seek escape from the challenges that the material world presented. On the contrary, his life was spent searching into the smallest details of the relationship between spirit and matter. This study enabled him to contribute significantly to the solution of a great number of important problems that had long baffled scientists.

Steiner was not satisfied with a one-sided picture of the human being that emphasized the spirit at the expense of the body or recognized only the body while denying the existence of the spirit. He saw in man's material embodiment evidence that the spirit required the enriching and developing experience possible in the realm of matter. But his observations convinced him that the spirit enters only slowly and gradually into its material counterpart, forming it by degrees into its perfect instrument. This process, he held, is one of such subtlety and complexity that those who would comprehend it must develop powers of observation of both a scientific and artistic kind. As he expressed it, "Science itself must become an art when we approach the secrets of man's being."

Education, in Rudolf Steiner's sense, was therefore an art as well as a science. In his approach to every educational problem he spoke as one in whom the artist-thinker, the psychologist and the physiologist were completely merged. He spoke at all times of the whole human being, of spirit, soul and body, and he conceived of education as a means whereby the slowly incarnating spirit could be helped to achieve a desirable harmony with the body.

In the various stages of bodily maturing Steiner saw evidence of the spirit's progressive mastery over its instrument. Physical changes thus became clues to a child's development, sensitive indicators to be closely noted by the teacher and followed by corresponding changes in educational procedure.

*   *   *   *   *   *

The first such change is the one that occurs at birth. The tiny baby issues forth from the protection of his mother's body into a world that at once begins to affect him. Tastes, sounds, smells, visual and tactual impressions storm in upon his slowly awakening senses. It is fortunate for him that their awakening takes place so gradually, for otherwise this sudden entrance into new surroundings might well prove a fatal shock.

Physically considered, the new-born child makes the impression of an unfinished symphony. His head is enormous and out of all proportion to the rest of his body, which seems to be merely a promise awaiting future fulfillment. He is as pliable as a piece of clay before it has been worked upon by the sculptor's will and set to harden in its final form.

But no sooner is he born than this will begins its activity. From the moment of birth—in fact, even during the latter part of his fetal development—he has an urge to movement. Throughout every waking hour he keeps up an astonishing ecstasy of chaotic motion, kicking and striking, beating his chest, flexing and unflexing leg, arm and finger muscles, pursing his lips, and making all manner of gestures with his vocal organs. An observer with a keen sense of the phenomenal will be struck by the drive and energy with which a baby carries on these activities. What can account for them? With adults, movement is always traceable to purposes. But can we legitimately speak of purposes in a new-born baby?

Obviously we cannot if by purpose we mean thought-directed impulses; the baby's every motion is chaotic. Yet if we watch him closely we shall find indisputable evidence of purpose in his gestures. He seems to be practicing something; he finds he has legs and arms and vocal organs, and he explores their possibilities with keenest interest. How exciting his discoveries are; how immense his pleasure in them! One is reminded of the first fumbling efforts of a puppeteer who stands behind the scenes of a puppet theater and attempts to control a

7

confusing group of strings. His is the natural awkwardness of a beginner. Just so does the human spirit, standing behind the scenes of its new-born body, embark upon the difficult task of controlling its organism. Slowly and surely order is wrought out of chaos.

Never again is a human being faced with a task as great as that which he accomplishes in his first three years of life. During this time his fresh spiritual energy is wholly given to the effort that transforms him from a helpless baby into a child who walks erect and speaks his thoughts in clearly formed sentences.

The sculptor has indeed been at work here! The head of the three-year-old has lost its first plastic softness. Its features have sharpened. The whole body takes on character and firmness. No longer does it appear an unfinished symphony; head, chest and limbs have reached more harmonious proportions.

Significant psychic changes have also taken place. The child of three has become a distinct individual. He calls himself "I," that name expressive of discovered selfhood. No longer is he content merely to eat, drink, sleep and make aimless motions. He has found himself in relation to his surroundings and continually reaches out to shape them more to his liking. He models his play on adult patterns, digging, building, looking at books and pictures, tending and scolding his dolls like a bossy parent. His incessant talk is the despair of grown-ups. It pours forth in torrents of questions to which any answer seems entirely satisfying.

Thoughtful observers will be struck by the comparatively slow pace with which the human child develops. Here we are confronted with a unique phenomenon of human evolution. Man, in whom as Goethe says, "Nature has brought creation to its loftiest peak," enters the world at birth as its most helpless creature. His form is less finished than that of any animal, his senses less awake. For weeks he lies oblivious of his surround-

8

ings. Young birds have flown before his eyes can f[
beavers have built their dams before he can sit al[
cats have brought forth kittens before he can wal[

Does he not seem the backward child of nature, r[....]than the most gifted of her offspring?

Yet at three, though still a baby he has already given evidence of possessing significant powers—the powers of thought, speech and upright carriage—that raise him far above the level of the animal. These human capacities require a longer period to ripen. Man is not to be hurried into premature adulthood. The human spirit, making its way into the alien element of earth, cannot at once lay hold upon the body provided by heredity. For years it must labor to remodel the inherited form into a shape more suited to its individual needs and character. With the cutting of the second teeth at six or seven this task is brought to completion.

Up to this time the spirit has worked almost wholly as a plastic artist, pouring its energy into the re-shaping of the bodily organism. The imitativeness of early childhood is a characteristic expression of this sculptural instinct. The child seizes eagerly on every impression and models himself upon it. He copies the people about him. He plays for hours at being the wind, a car, a wave, an animal. Everything moving and sounding attracts his attention and is imitated. The sculptor in him delights in making mud pies, building sand castles, forming all sorts of figures out of clay or dough. Let him into the kitchen to cut out cookies or to make a gingerbread boy and he will be your friend for life! His hands long for opportunities to pat things into shape.

In this imitative period the child's whole future is profoundly influenced by the nature of the people about him. Their inmost qualities, reflected in speech, thought and gesture, affect him deeply. Psychologists have long been aware of this important fact. They tell us that a child's early human en-

9

vironment is the most formative factor in his development. He may be likened to a plant, dependent for his growth upon the fertile or barren soil of the adult community. Steiner's researches convinced him that even bodily health is affected by impressions received during childhood. The damage done may not show for many years, but bad impressions nevertheless bring about subtle disorders in the child's highly sensitive organism that later result in illness.

It is essential that we know these things. Only a clear insight into the inter-relationship of spirit, soul and body can suffice to guide us in providing the child with the environment he needs for a wholesome development.

* * * * * *

With the coming of the second teeth significant changes may be noted in the child's whole being. He is no longer so absorbed in sense impressions. To a certain extent he has separated himself from the outer world, and lives more withdrawn in an inner world of feeling. He becomes more thoughtful and reserved. When he asks us a question he listens carefully to our reply.

In this second phase of development the child is no longer a creature of blind, chaotic will that impels him to ceaseless limb activity. The energy that was so lately poured into the forming of his physical organism is now freed for other efforts. It reappears transformed as an enhanced capacity for thought and feeling.

This inner development takes place at the expense of the body. Recent tests have brought out the fact that physical endurance is actually at its maximum in the child of six, gradually decreasing through the rest of life. Though bodily growth continues, it does so at a slower pace. Head, chest and limbs have realigned themselves in new proportions.

Breathing and blood circulation, too, have outgrown the swift tempo of early childhood and settled down into calmer motion. Their steady rhythms make the child's body seem like an instrument in perfect tune. A musical sense awakens in him. He loves to sing, dance, recite and to play games such as "Here we go 'round the mulberry bush," "London Bridge is falling down," or "A trisket, a trasket, a green and yellow basket"—games in which his new rhythmic talents may be exercised.

Now he is ready to enter school. What a shock it is if his teacher, who might guide him to the discovery of a world of beauty, has nothing to offer but the driest sort of learning! At first even the dullest studies have the charm of novelty, but soon that wears off, and he is left disillusioned with his schooling.

Though his fantasy is no longer quite so riotous, the child of six is still a dreamer. His thinking has an imaginative rather than an abstract character. He is incapable of absorbing intellectual concepts. If they are forced upon him he will feel like the man in Grimm's nightmarish story who found himself sleeping with a corpse. Dead knowledge chills and repels him. His need is for learning of a warm and vital kind that can engage his feeling and lead him out beyond himself into a stirring experience of beauty.

During this second period, the child is an instinctive artist. He delights in contrast. To paint red beside blue fills him with pleasure. He lives deeply in the rhythmic, alternating seasons, of day and night, of rain and sunshine. He loves to hear stories in which beautiful princesses are rescued from ugly dragons, or a loathsome frog turns out to be a king's son in disguise. A song that modulates from major into minor, changes its tempo, or alternates between forte and piano will please him especially.

Not only does he delight in perceiving beauty; he loves to

11

create it. During this period his teacher will do well to shape each lesson on a rhythmic pattern in which listening or looking is balanced by the child's own activity in doing.

* * * * * *

As he approaches puberty, further changes occur in the child's physical and psychic make-up. His growth becomes more rapid, his arms and legs lengthen alarmingly, and his thinking powers are strengthened to a marked degree. Mental concepts begin to acquire a real meaning for him. Now he can be introduced to the physical sciences, which at an earlier age remained quite beyond his comprehension.

The Swiss psychologist Piaget has presented interesting evidence of this change in the child's thought processes. In his interviews with a great number of children he discovered that up to the age of twelve or thereabouts they believed that their thinking was done with the larynx, the mouth, or the ears, not with the brain. Their thoughts were experienced as "a silent voice." They were unconscious of possessing a mind. Thoughts came to them from outside as pictures that were changed into words in the mouth where they were experienced. Only at eleven or twelve did they begin to conceive of thinking as an adult does.

At puberty the child is no longer a dreamer with an imaginative way of perceiving the world about him. He has "come to himself" and is wide awake. Whereas formerly it was his feeling that stirred and quickened to his experiences, now his thinking is challenged by every happening.

If, before the change of teeth, the child has developed wholesomely among adults whose character has provided him with impressions of moral strength; if, between second dentition and puberty, his teacher has been an artist able to satisfy his need of beauty, the child enters adolescence with a thought capacity powered by a healthy will, warmed and enriched by feeling.

* * * * * *

Past generations of teachers spoke of education as a means of "preparing the child for life." Modern educators are not in sympathy with this aim. When, they ask, does "life" begin? Is it not constantly being lived? They state their objective differently. It is "to give children meaningful experience at every age."

A true art of education can reconcile these seemingly conflicting purposes. It founds its practices upon an insight into the changing interplay of body, soul and spirit in the different periods of the child's development. It sees in the child from birth to the change of teeth a being of wholly different needs than those of the second period, which terminates in puberty, or of the third, when the child becomes an adult. In the first of these three phases it recognizes a predominance of physical activity, outwardly manifest in the body's swift growth and the will to motion; in the second, a predominance of soul or feeling, manifest in the child's new capacity for aesthetic experience; and in the third, a predominance of the spirit, manifest in the abstract thinking and independent judgment of which the child now becomes capable. With the ending of this third phase of development, body, soul and spirit have come into balance. We speak of young people of twenty-one as "having reached their majority." They are now indeed "prepared for life" and ready to enter it, as they were not before this time.

At each stage of growth the education proper to body, soul and spirit, to will, feeling and thought, gives children the truest kind of "meaningful experience." They will not have to search themselves to discover what their needs are. These needs will have been anticipated by the teacher's insight.

The educational ideal of the Pragmatists—the activity program—most conforms to the needs of the first, essentially physical period of development; that of the Idealists—beauty—to the needs of the second; that of the Realists—disciplined thought and observation—to the needs of the third.

Though these three periods are clearly marked, the transition from one to the other is long in preparation. Months, or even years, go by before it is accomplished. Yet when the moment is ripe the physiological and psychic symptoms of change make their appearance almost overnight. Observant parents and teachers have often had the startling experience of waking up one morning to be confronted by a changeling of unfamiliar appearance and capacities.

The metamorphoses whereby the physical energy of early childhood is slowly transformed into the inner energy of feeling, whereby thought in turn is later born of feeling-energy, are subtle processes. They must be helped, not forced. It should be the ideal of the teacher to assist the child in the second growth period to disengage his feeling from the life of will and to attach it to thinking. If this is accomplished the child is steadied through the emotional awakening of adolescence. He is helped to reach maturity at twenty-one as a complete, harmoniously developed human being.

This is the goal that the new art of education sets itself.

CHAPTER II

The Six-Year-Olds

It is surprising to discover how few adults have any recollection of their first day at school. Though this event is usually one of the most vivid of a lifetime's experience, it is often allowed—perhaps even forced—to sink deep into oblivion. But it has nonetheless had its profoundly formative effect.

The first day of school is like a bridge leading from a life of free, spontaneous activity in the intimate surroundings of home and neighborhood into another different world where the child takes part in an organized experience of learning. Traditionally, it has been a bridge of sighs leading to a dreadful death, or at best many years' imprisonment. But it can be made to lead to a world of large adventure such as the heart of any child will thrill to. It will depend entirely upon the teacher what sort of impression the child crossing this bridge is given, and upon his reaction depends his future attitude toward life and learning.

The child goes to school not wholly unprepared for the work he is now to embark on, for he has been hard at play for several years. Anyone who has seen him at it knows that playing has been as strenuous an activity, as serious a profession as any to which adult life could call him. It has been his whole-souled labor, pursued with a concentration rarely seen except in childhood. But there is an essential difference between his play and the work of adults: the child's play springs from spontaneous inner impulse, whereas the adult's work is with few exceptions dictated from without by the needs of society.

Into the organized work and society of the schoolroom the child now enters. The transition is indeed a marked one. But he need not be coddled through it in a mistaken policy of sugar-coating the supposedly bitter pill of learning and making his work mere play, for it is no longer play that he most craves. If he has not entered school before there are sure signs of his readiness, he will be genuinely eager to take the steps natural to his new capacities, to enter a wider world, to take part in organized group experience, to attain the scholar's dignity that now becomes him.

But if his activity should not remain mere child's play, neither should it become, as so often happens, a premature plunging into the element of adult knowledge. There is a middle ground entirely suited to this second phase of the child's maturation, to the imaginative quality of his thinking, to his need to have his whole being engaged in learning. This ground is that of art, for art is both play and knowledge, fact heightened and revealed by beauty, a living form of truth. Art enlivens all it touches; art brings the static into motion; art educates to wholeness. The teacher who would be equal to his task as his pupils come to him for their first day of school experience must therefore be one who has the artist's magic touch and who knows how to use it to endow every aspect of his subject matter with life and beauty. If he cannot do so, he has no choice but to burden his pupils with a crushing weight of purely external skills and lifeless knowledge such as they are traditionally required to master in the eight short years of elementary schooling. Such a course is catastrophic for the child's development. It means an abrupt breaking off of play activity followed by a crippling blitzkrieg on the intellect, which is caught defenseless in the very cradle. Only an artistically conceived education can avoid these dangers. Such an education provides the natural bridge from play to work and relieves the learning process of an alien intellectual element.

* * * * * *

A child's readiness to begin his schooling, indicated by the significant breaking through of the second teeth, offers the teacher both support and challenge as he opens school on the first morning with a brief assembly. The children confronting him are aware that they are entering upon a new, more mature phase of their experience. They are eager to learn. They have a deep-felt need to be taken seriously in this desire. Such an attitude on their part enables the teacher to speak to them on the occasion of their first school encounter in a way that will be welcome and make a profound impression. He will do well to begin by speaking of their presence in the schoolroom as evidence of a purpose shared in common: They have come to work and learn together. And he will speak of the wonderful things that people have already learned to do in the world and of the many other wonderful things that still remain to be explored and done. He will remind the children how they have seen their fathers and mothers and other grown-ups reading and writing, telling time, and using numbers. Now they themselves are old enough to be able to learn to do these things.

This opening note may perhaps seem superfluous. Yet it has great significance for the children. It links their present to both past and future. It places their learning in perspective and gives it all the more import. They are falling heir to treasures that are the product of generations of cultural laborers. There is great social value as well as realism in making them aware that the skills and knowledge they inherit are the fruits of long effort and worthy of their deepest veneration. This theme should be vividly dwelt upon.

17

But their attention should also be directed to the future, which is to be of their shaping. It will therefore be wholesome to speak of this first day at school as the beginning of a new life, a life in which they will learn to do many things they cannot yet do and to take part in the work of the world. To look ahead to distant goals and to reach out toward them strengthens the child's will and sharpens his sense of purpose.

After touching on these matters delicately yet impressively—perhaps telling a story that clothes them in speaking pictures—the teacher will do well to change his tone and proceed to the lively activities that will be part of every day's experience. These are well-named opening exercises designed to awaken the child to his tiptoes and concentrate him before his work begins. Traditionally, opening exercises have been dull affairs made up of perfunctory prayer and a half-hearted mumbling of songs and poems. But in Steiner schools they serve an important function, and care is taken to make them vital. Like all other "periods" they must achieve a well-rounded balance by including a wide variety of experiences. There must be solemn as well as gay moments, quiet looking and listening as well as vigorous motor activity, learning something new as well as repeating more familiar material. There is no set program to be followed, however, with the single exception of the opening poem, recited in lieu of a prayer.* This is important for the mood of reverence and purpose it awakens. It should never be allowed to lapse into mere routine. The teacher's sincerity in speaking the words does much to keep them meaningful for the children.

*   *   *   *   *   *

*The poem used for the first three grades was composed by Dr. Steiner and reads as follows:

18

In addition to speech and musical experiences certain eurythmy exercises are included in the program. These have the function of harmonizing will, thought, and feeling. They will be considered below in a discussion of curative eurythmy.

The effect of the opening exercises should be twofold: to prepare the children to begin their work in an active, concentrated spirit, and to build class unity. If the material is well-chosen, the children will take a deep esthetic pleasure in it. They love to sing, play, act, move and recite together. There is no satisfaction to be compared with that of stimulating group activity, no fellowship freer or warmer than that built up in communal experience in creating beauty.

Once the teacher has provided the children with an initial extensive repertory they will take a highly active part in shaping the class assembly programs, drawing on familiar material as well as bringing in new songs, poems and stories. The teacher may gauge his progress as an artist and leader very largely by the eagerness with which the children enter into these assemblies.

After these daily exercises the children go on to what is known as the main lesson period. This occupies the first two

---

◁

The sun, with loving light,
Brings brightness to my day.
The soul, with spirit might,
Pours strength into my limbs.
In sunlight shining clear
I reverence, O God,
The strength of human kind
Which Thou so graciously
Hast planted in my soul
That I may love to work
And learn with all my might.
From Thee come strength and light;
To Thee rise love and thanks.
                    (Translation)

19

hours of the morning and is devoted to a single subject for a stretch of from two to six, or even eight weeks' duration.

It may no longer be necessary to defend this practice, which at the time of its introduction at the Waldorf School in 1919 seemed radical to many. In the light of our present deeper understanding of human psychology one may perhaps rather question how any such indefensible arrangement as the traditional succession of forty minute periods ever found its way into favor. Such a practice completely disregards human nature and the laws of learning. To expose a child or adult to an interest in some activity only to tear him away from it after a few minutes and plunge him into another is to discourage all natural interest in learning and to turn healthy human beings into nervous cripples. The Waldorf plan, in assigning the greater part of the morning to concentration in a single area, avoids the disruption and superficiality inherent in the forty-minute schedule. It allows for an easy, deep-breathing absorption, an unhurried exploration of a subject's many facets. When, in a matter of weeks, the children's interest has been satisfied and begins to slacken, what possibilities of refreshment lie in turning to an entirely new sphere of experience! Here variety is used on a large scale, wholesomely, rather than with the short-term overstimulation of which schools are so often guilty. When the teacher working with the Waldorf plan turns from one subject field to another, he chooses the subject that in his estimation offers the most refreshing contrast possible. In the meantime the experiences reaped from the subject temporarily dropped from the curriculum are allowed to sink into seeming oblivion. But in reality they lie in a state of fallow resting from which they will one day spring up with greater vigor in a riper form. This kind of forgetting, far from being dreaded, is positively encouraged as a prime educational ally in schools that have adopted the Waldorf plan. It has been found that a short recapitulation of the material so "forgotten" suffices for its retention in a far more vivid and growing form than if it had been kept constantly in view throughout the term.

The question may arise whether a two-hour period is not too exhausting for the children. This cannot be the case, due to a basic ordering of each lesson that provides for a threefold activity within every such period. In accordance with human nature, which lives quite differently in thinking, feeling, and willing or motor experiences, activities of the period strike a rhythmic balance between mental effort, artistic creation, and motor activity. Yet all three experiences are centered in a single natural field of interest called a subject.

It is surprising to a teacher new to this main lesson period to find how quickly the two hours that seemed so long in prospect really pass. As for the children, they are taken by surprise almost every day when they are told that it is time to go out to recess. Even after two hours they are seldom ready to stop working. Sighs of relief on their part are an unfailing indication that the teacher's planning of the lesson has lacked balance.

The sequence in which subjects are chosen for the main lesson is a matter for each teacher's own decision. Factors of many kinds make freedom of choice imperative. Only in the first grade will there be unanimity, and this is dictated by practical considerations. Every first grade teacher takes painting and drawing as the first main lesson subject, continuing it until the children have a certain facility in handling crayons, paints and paint-brush. Their reason for beginning with this activity is its relation to all other first grade learning. As will appear below, reading, writing, number, nature study and handwork are all taught in ways involving the use of color and design.

A story may well precede adventuring with colors. To prosaic adults the pots of color set before the children may seem to

21

contain nothing more than pigments to be transferred to paper in simulation of various external objects. But actually these pots are full of magic: carmine, royal as a king; vermillion, roaring out angry challenges; a gently gleaming yellow like a sun in miniature; the soft blue of noonday; and ultramarine, deep, remote and peaceful as the starry heavens. Each color waits, patiently or otherwise according to its nature, to be released from the confinement of its pot and allowed free movement. Carmine advances warmly and majestically, vermillion leaps fiercely forward on the paper; the blues retire into the background, creating the illusion of great distances; yellow sends its shining rays in all directions. Each one is a vivid personality, alive and active, lending itself easily to the weaving of a thousand stories. But the stories told at the beginning of a painting lesson are not primarily themes for illustration. They are rather means whereby the child is made more keenly aware of the life and mood of color, of the part colors play in the drama of a picture's composition.

Goethe, who devoted many years to color studies, spoke of colors as "the deeds of light," as movement and gesture. Children naturally experience color in this dynamic way. Stories woven around characters whose qualities literally *color* the narrative heighten the child's natural sense of color as a dynamic element. They help to preclude any possibility that he will ever lose it. There is nothing sadder than to find adults looking upon colors as static layers of pigment attached to the outer surfaces of things.

It is essential to a pure experience of color that clear fluid paints be used. Poster paints with their gravy-like consistency and crude hues can never be a satisfactory substitute for water color, which, when it is applied on white paper, suggests the mobile freedom and transparency of light itself.

No set themes should be given painters who are having their first adventure in the realm of color. They must be free to

22

explore, to let the reds, blues and yellow run over the paper striking up acquaintance, mixing, blending or battling, revealing themselves differently in every new relationship and bringing more and more colors into being through their meetings.

There are many hazards to be overcome in water color painting, hazards that often discourage its use for young children and so deprive them of this purest of color experiences. These hazards are the physical difficulties of controlling the medium. There is no choice for the teacher but to take this problem by the horns and apply patience and thoroughness to its solution. It is rewarding to find that first-graders quickly grow accustomed to the difficulties and with practice soon overcome them. They must be taught to wet and stretch their paper on the boards, to avoid overloading their brushes, and to wash them before dipping them into another pot of color. All this soon becomes quite automatic. Many accidents are bound to happen in the first few lessons. But they should be treated lightly and never allowed to dampen the spirits of the young painters.

In working with this flowing medium the children find that where one area of color impinges on another, lines and forms come into being. This discovery leads them naturally into drawing. Great care should be taken at this moment to keep the children from falling into an inartistic and widespread habit of conceiving of form as filled-in outline. Psychologists of the future will have a hard time accounting for this strange aberration so prevalent in our time. It is certainly a sign of the unreality that has crept into our perceptive faculty. We seem to see even physical objects abstractly, for no body in the whole realm of nature was ever built from an outline inward; quite the opposite. Yet school art has always followed this unnatural procedure in teaching the technique of drawing. As a result of their painting experience the children in Steiner schools learn to know color as a moving element, and line as the border of moving color masses. Their drawing, which in the primary grades is always done with paint brush or colored crayons, is thus built on a mobile rather than a static sense of line.

But drawing is made an activity for more than just hand and eye. The child's whole body shares in the form experience as he moves on straight and round lines drawn on the floor of his classroom, and learns to feel the difference between plastic curving and the unyielding sword-thrust rigidity of straightness. The most varied designs of straight and curving lines are made by moving groups, linking the sense of form with the sense of movement.

From these beginnings in color and design the children go on to make simple pictures, using both paints and crayons. At this age the emphasis should be on the color experience rather than on achieving external resemblances. Fortunately, children in the primary grades are seldom troubled by the feelings of incapacity that so often plague adults in their first approach to the arts. Children have a naive delight in color, a love of dramatic portraiture that flows with uncanny ease into expression. With a little help and practice they can usually surpass all but the most talented of teachers.

*   *   *   *   *   *

From these initial color and form experiences, which occupy the main lesson period for the first week or two, the children go on to a longer series of main lessons in the art of writing.

Adults, to whom the use of letter symbols has become second nature, can hardly appreciate what a dismaying impression these strange skeletal figures must make on children, what unassimilable morsels they must seem in the learning diet. But they need not remain an entirely alien element. The history of writing shows that letter forms first came into being as pictures. We shall see below in a discussion of eurythmy that the very life of speech has been conjured into these symbols. If they

24

are presented in a lively pictorial way they will be fraught with imaginative qualities that avoid the burdensome aspects of learning to write and instead greatly enrich the child's whole school experience.

This is done with the help of fairy stories. The teacher may choose an ancient tale like "The Fisherman's Wife" for his purpose. He tells the story vividly, describing the raging wind, the heaving sea and the fisherman's boat bobbing up and down like a cork on the billows. No sooner has the fisherman cast his net into the water than a huge fish is struggling in its meshes. On being pulled into the boat the fish speaks and begs the fisherman to set him free, saying that he is a king and a magician who will buy his ransom by fulfilling any wish the fisherman expresses. The fisherman makes his wish, lets the fish go and rows home to find his humble hut transformed into a princely dwelling and his hard working wife proudly sitting at ease by the parlor fire. The story continues to its dramatic close. When it is finished, the teacher takes colored chalks and draws a picture on the blackboard showing the stormy waters and the fisherman in his boat talking over the side to the fish, who wears a crown and is in the act of slipping back into the deep from a heaving wave-crest. While he draws, the children take colored crayons and make pictures of their own in which waves, fish and fisherman appear. The teacher then draws the children's attention to the fact that when they speak the words "wind, water, wave" and other words that begin with the same sound there is the same fine upsurging heaving in the sound as in the wave forms pictured in the drawing. The F sound too has its own peculiar character. It flips, flits, flashes, floats and flies away with the same finicky, flickering "here-one-moment-and-gone-the-next" fickleness of motion with which fishes dart through the fluid element. The children delight in practicing the sounds and finding more words of the same kind. Soon the motion of the sounds themselves has turned them into waves and fishes, and they move around the schoolroom carried by these dynamic F's and W's. After they have practiced awhile and have the feel of the sounds and their motion tingling through them the teacher tells them how grown-ups have come to call the wave sound by the name "W" and the flitting sound "F." He thus distinguishes between the sound as a dynamic force and the name given it in conventional usage. Then, on his blackboard drawing, he shows how the wave forms are W's and the fish with his fins an F. He writes down the words that the children have found to begin with these sounds. The children then make a page of printed capital F's and W's in their writing books beside the illustration they have just drawn there. First, however, they draw the letters in the air with their hands and on the floor as a large pattern to move on with their feet. So every part of them has its share in the writing experience.

Other stories on the other days provide other sound and form motives, until the children have learned all the letters of the alphabet. S may be a fairy tale snake sinuously slithering through the grass on some secret errand, M a twin-peaked mountain thrusting skyward, Q a queen with a love of long trains, and so on. The child is introduced not only to writing, but to the secret of speech, which is hidden movement. He acquires a rich treasure of pictorial impressions to nourish his imagination. Instead of being drained of his vitality in an effort to digest a foreign element, he is given experiences that enhance it. Every bit of him—head, heart and limbs—is engaged in the learning process. When he has mastered the sounds and can name and write them, first as printed capitals and then in their small printed form, he is ready for his first reading experiences. These must be given in a way that has real meaning for him.

The children may be asked to repeat a favorite story, or the teacher may tell them a new one. The episodes of the story are then illustrated by a series of pictures drawn in daily succession on the blackboard by the teacher and in their notebooks by the children. The class composes one or two short descriptive sentences, or better still a verse, to accompany each picture as it is finished. The wording is then copied in colored pencil from the teacher's model. Such composition offers an opportunity to cultivate the poetic sense through choosing the most beautiful wording possible, and the children are not likely to have difficulty reading sentences that they have written themselves with such loving care.

Through these activities the children learn word and sentence structure without conscious effort and have the joy of creating their own illustrated books for reading material. It is not long before they are reading other simple stories. But there is a great dearth of books that can compare with the children's own in beauty of wording and illustration, and the transition from school-made books to purchased readers is therefore something of a problem. The teacher can help by adding creations of his own to the class library. At this age it is of the greatest importance that every impression the children receive be fraught with beauty, and no effort should be spared to make this possible.

*　*　*　*　*　*

Numbers come next, and occupy an extended series of main lessons. Probably no subject holds greater terrors for most school children. Attempts to make it more human and interesting by centering arithmetic around the children's own practical problems have done little to remedy the situation. It is not difficult to see why. To keep numbers in a purely utilitarian category is to keep them forever at arm's length. Of course, they are useful, but this is not the whole story. Numbers were not invented by man to suit his practical convenience, they were *discovered* realities! They are built into the very structure of man and the universe. They are rhythm and movement, design, color, tone and form, not dusty counters as the arithmetic books would have us believe.

One of the most fascinating things about numbers is the element of contrast it offers the imagination. Think of a field containing something as finite, concrete, specific and concentrated as the number 1 and at the same time capable of numbers so huge as to be quite beyond conceiving! Even to hint at such possibilities in a fairy tale where an enchanter with a magic wand easily makes numerical mountains out of molehills awes the children deeply. It makes them feel from the first that they are dealing with a mobile element.

The exploration of numbers can begin with a riddle: What is the one thing in the whole wide world that there can never be more than one of? The children are at once intrigued. They become inwardly active as they search for the answer. Can it be that book, or this flower, or your suit? No, there could be many other books, flowers and suits just like these. They look all around the classroom and out the windows. Suddenly it will occur to someone to discover himself and shout, "Me!" This is a significant moment for all the children, this discovery of individual uniqueness, and the teacher can show that grownups write the figure one exactly like "I," the symbol for the name by which we each call ourselves.

Now he can go on to two-ness and ask the children to name all the pairs of opposites they can think of, such as day and night, sun and moon, boy and girl, rain and shine, and so on. He can show how these two opposites may be drawn as two opposite curves, or for even greater contrast, with one curve and one straight line, as in the figure 2.

So one may proceed with all the figures, finding a picturing of number-qualities as well as quantities in every symbol, or telling a fairy story to be illustrated with a form-motif that leads to the number-symbol as was done in teaching the letters of the alphabet. As each figure is learned, the children practice writing it in many ways. They form it with their hands in the air; they draw it with huge lines in colored chalk on the blackboard; they run it with their feet as a floor pattern. Finally, they write it with colored pencils in their arithmetic notebooks, which are already bright with story illustrations.

But stories and riddles are only a small part of first grade number experiences. Another great surprise and pleasure lies in discovering the wealth of numbers hidden in one's own body—the things that come in ones, in pairs, in fours, fives, tens and twenties. Then there are geometric figures to go with each number; circles, crosses, triangles, squares, five-pointed stars, and so on. One can even become a five-pointed star oneself by holding one's head erect and stretching out arms and legs. All these figures are marked on the floor and the blackboard, moved on, and then transferred to paper.

There is immense delight in simply counting, especially when the strong rhythmic choral-speaking of the numbers is accompanied by rhythmic stepping or clapping. How good it is to hear the numbers growing bigger and bigger and following each other in such ordered sequences!

Then there are the possibilities of dancing to numbers. By bringing accents into the counting: "one, *two*; three, *four*; five, *six*, seven, *eight*" or "one, two, *three*; four, five, *six*; seven, eight, *nine*; ten, eleven, *twelve*", one is made to step softly on the unaccented syllables and hard on the accented ones, or to take little light running steps followed by a fine long leap on the accents. Some can play their flutes by way of accompaniment, toot-tooting instead of counting.

Through activities such as these the children befriend themselves with the form and movement of the number element. When they are sufficiently at home in it, they may begin to practice with the four arithmetical processes. Here, too, stories in which a number-motif occurs provide ideal beginning material. Fairy tales like "The Twelve Dancing Princesses" or "The Seven Swans" are rich in opportunities to add, subtract, divide and multiply. At first sheer headwork cannot be expected of the children. They will therefore be given pinecones, acorns, marbles or other small objects to serve as counters.

In using the four processes in number games or stories a vital educational principle—that of proceeding from wholes to parts rather than atomistically from parts to wholes—is faithfully observed. The twelve dancing princesses may cross the lake in several boatloads to the place where their night's entertainment awaits them. Then 12 may equal 4 and 4 and 4, or 4 times 3, or 5 and 4 and 3, and so on. Perhaps one night two pairs of especially eager princesses will finish putting on their beautiful ball dresses before the others and hurry on ahead, leaving all the rest to cross in one tippy boatload, in which case 12 equals 2 and 2 and 8. Or one slow-poke may be left behind, in which case 12 minus 1 equals 11. The dramatic possibilities are infinite and may be spun out in the most colorful fashion. The children are counters as they act out the stories and check on the arithmetical results. To begin with, no distinctions are made between the four processes, though all four are applied concretely. The counters are pooled at the beginning of every new example and then moved as the story requires. Only after considerable practical experience in adding, subtracting, multiplying and dividing does the teacher introduce the symbols for these operations.

Again notebooks are made and illustrated, and examples of all kinds are entered in them in connection with each story. In every case the whole number is written first—the sum before the addends, the product before the multiplicand and multiplier, and so on, in order that the method of proceeding from wholeness shall become habitual.

* * * * * *

Nature study, too, has its share of main lessons, for the role played by this subject in the child's development is an important one. It has the task of awakening him to a more conscious experiencing of the world around him.

During his first six years of life the child has been in and of the world of nature and enjoyed it quite naively. Indeed, he has been so much a part of nature as scarcely to distinguish between himself and nature's beings and events. His felt oneness with the world has moved him to constant imitation. If a dog barked or a bird flew, he felt that he barked and flew too. He was the rain raining, the sun shining, the flying cloud, the wind. He sprouted and opened with the flowers. Every gesture of nature was something in which he felt his being moving and gesturing. But the significant turning point that has been passed in his development now enables him to stand aside and look at the world more objectively.

But it would be harmful to plunge him in his still dreaming state of consciousness directly into "realistic" natural science. This would mean too harsh, too abrupt a transition. He is not yet ready for scientific impersonality. The world about him still seems very much alive. To him, everything that moves and changes is a person like himself, though not in a crude external sense. He feels so intensely that he endows all nature with feeling. His first introduction to nature study, therefore, takes the form of an experience of hearing the world speak to him and tell him about its life and adventures. He learns the true facts of nature, but always in vivid and dramatic form. He may, for example, be told the life story of a drop of moisture. He hears how it first found itself sailing along with many fellow-travelers in a big white cloud driven by a strong wind through the summer sky. Far, far below on the earth lay a great mountain, shimmering like silver in the heat of noon. The plants that grew on the mountainside were withering and crying out for water. So down dashed the drops in floods of cooling rain

31

to their rescue. Each drop sank deep into the hard, sun-baked, parched ground where the roots were growing and brought them water. Then came a long journey through the darkness, until at last one fine summer morning our raindrop and some of his companions made their way out into the daylight on a sloping hillside. How good it was to be free again! They ran races down the mountainside in their delight. Other drops joined them. Now there were so many that they made a tiny brook. At every turn more drops fell in, until soon the little brook became a big stream rushing and brawling down the mountain and leaping high over stones and boulders. Animals came out of the forest to drink in the quiet pools where some drops stayed. As the stream hurried on it met other streams and grew steadily larger. Finally it reached a broad plain and became a great slowly flowing river. Now boats came from the ocean and sailed up and down along it carrying great loads of things to the people who lived along its banks. Now it was not long before the drops saw the shining ocean lying far ahead. They began to taste its salty waters, which flowed up and mingled with them. So their long journey ended for a time at least, until once again the sun shone so strongly that great numbers of drops climbed upwards toward him in floating clouds of mist to set sail on another airy voyage.

A presentation such as this borrows its drama from reality, from the actual cyclic movement of the watery element. It captures the child's whole-hearted interest. Such pictures convey never-to-be-forgotten impressions. When, several years later, the children begin their scientific studies and learn to know nature from another side, these impressions remain with them as a warm experience of knowledge, as a still subtly re-echoing overtone of beauty.

In similar fashion plants, stones and animals may be allowed to speak poetically about themselves. Hills, sky, sun, moon and stars, winds, rivers, forests—and mother earth herself—may all reveal something of themselves in appropriate images. The series of nature lessons should be made to culminate in vivid impressions of the rhythm, the majestic harmony with which nature has imbued her handiwork. Such impressions do more to build moral strength and to foster a sense of social responsibility than any amount of preaching or talk of cooperation.

Lessons such as these offer opportunity for many kinds of experience. The teacher does not simply sit and lecture. Plays are written and enacted, paintings made, dances danced. There is singing, reciting and story-telling. All these activities arise naturally out of the subject matter, ordering the lessons in a variety of rhythmic patterns.

* * * * * *

According to the Waldorf School plan the three R's or "academic" studies such as the above are assigned to the main lesson period in blocks of varying length. This means that the greater part of the morning is given to activities centering in one subject-field. When the main lesson period is over the children have recess. On their return they are given shorter periods of instruction in other subject matter that offers a decided contrast to the experiences of the first part of the morning. Among these are two foreign languages, eurythmy, singing and handwork.

The two foreign languages are of course chosen for their appropriateness to the time and the school's location. Each language is given at least two weekly periods of about an hour's duration.

The imitative genius characteristic of early childhood is still sufficiently active in primary children to make their first three years of schooling the most ideal time to learn foreign languages. The speech organs, like the child's whole body, are

33

still highly plastic, making the acquiring of a native accent possible. The language teachers are chosen for their purity of accent, among other important qualifications. This is a prime consideration because of the method used.

In the first three grades the children learn languages entirely through hearing and speaking them. Poems are learned by heart and recited, songs are sung, action games are played and dramas enacted. The children's attention is thus wholly given to the sound and "feel" of the language rather than to the meaning of this or that single word. They do not see the language written, nor does the teacher do any but the most sparse and general translating in order that their approach to the language shall be a fresh and complete experience rather than an atomistic piecing together of single words and phrases.

This method has been found most effective in leading the children deep into the heart of a language. It enables them to have a direct experience of another folk-element as this is vividly revealed in the characteristic rhythms, sounds, and even the melody of a people's speech.

* * * * *

Handwork may be taken either as a short series of main lessons or twice weekly for one-hour periods, or both. This will vary with the varying activities. Modelling and drawing practice, for example, may safely be given longer periods than knitting, which is apt to tire the children quickly.

Handwork, especially in the primary grades, serves a number of important purposes. There exists a close though as yet not widely recognized relationship between finger-movement, speech and thinking. Steiner, who discovered this relationship, pointed out its developmental and corrective implications to the Waldorf teachers. Their experience, as well as my own, has fully borne out Steiner's statement that nimble fingers make for clear-cut speech and lively thinking. Children whose preschool activities have been such as to make their hands clever, their fingers dexterous, will be found to articulate clearly and do nimble thinking. Conversely, clumsy-handed children are clumsy-tongued and clumsy-headed. Much can be done in the primary grades with handwork to help overcome this clumsiness. Knitting, which makes special demands on the fingers, is therefore an indispensable first grade activity. It should be done with large needles and thick, brightly colored strands of wool or string.

Modelling too is of first importance. It may be wise to introduce it early in the year in a short series of main lesson periods as is done in the case of painting. Modelling may also be done in connection with writing lessons, nature study and arithmetic. Handwork periods are often set aside for modelling to ensure plenty of finger work.

In the first three grades it is advisable to provide colored beeswax rather than clay or plastilene as modelling material, for these inorganic substances are subtly repellent to children in a period of development when their whole concern is with life and living things. Lifeless material may dampen their pleasure in modelling. Real beeswax, if it is to be had, is ideal, and it has the added attraction of the honey fragrance. To children living as deeply in sense impressions as they do at this age such factors are by no means negligible.

Primary children should always model whole scenes taken from story experiences rather than single figures. At this age their attention is on relationships rather than isolated persons or animals.

Drawing with colored chalks or pencils is also excellent eye and finger training which may find a place in handwork periods. Exercises in symmetry will delight the children especially. A paper is folded down the middle and the teacher draws one half of a geometric or curving design to one side of this

35

symmetry axis. The child then completes it on the other side of the axis. Such exercises greatly aid concentration and will be found wonderfully helpful in overcoming constitutional nervousness.

Music periods in the primary grades are devoted to singing and to playing the recorder flute. This latter activity is one that also helps develop finger dexterity. All the children learn to play this instrument; it is surprising how quickly they master it. Drums, triangles and other percussion instruments are also introduced into music lessons.

Like all other subject matter in the Steiner curriculum, music is taught as a means of full and wholesome development rather than for the sake of acquiring skills and a repertory. This art is peculiarly suited to the needs of children in the second growth phase when the feeling life, which was heretofore closely bound up with the life of the will and hence with bodily activity, loosens its connection with the will to attach itself more to the inward life of thought. For music is the most inward of the arts. It speaks to depths that can be reached in no other way; depths of human nature find expression through it that would otherwise never be revealed. To create or to hear music is to experience beauty most directly. It is the most personal and at the same time one of the most social of the arts. It has a profoundly refining, ennobling effect upon those who open themselves to its influence. As Shakespeare says, (Merchant of Venice, V, I):

> The man that hath no music in himself
> Nor is not moved with concord of sweet sounds;
> Is fit for treasons, strategems and spoils;
> Let no such man be trusted.

Every child in a Steiner school is given wide experience in hearing and making music in order that his feeling be enriched and cultivated and the most noble qualities of human nature strengthened in him.

Like all rhythmic activities, music is a means whereby the child's whole being may be harmonized. The teacher who understands how to give music its rightful place in the curriculum will be astonished to see how quickly changes are wrought in the expressions and behavior of his pupils.

First grade music lessons should strike a nice balance between listening and doing. No attempt is made to teach notation or theory of any kind. Singing is a purely esthetic experiencing of melody, harmony and rhythm. Flute lessons acquaint the children with their instruments, and simple tunes within one octave are learned by watching the teacher's fingering and playing with him. Both singing and fluting are given two half-hour periods weekly.

English, or language study, is not given special periods in the first grade curriculum; it plays too basic a part in every other study to be isolated. There is the wealth of stories told in connection with the main lessons and re-told by the children, the poems learned and recited during the daily assembly, the songs, the letters, the reading. And there are speech exercises, jolly alliterations, practiced every morning in the opening exercises to accustom the children to speak clearly and beautifully and to feel the potent life of sounds. Lastly, there is the teacher's own profound realization of the formative power of speech, which causes him to use speech at all times as an artist in language.

* * * * * *

Eurythmy, which comes last to mention, pervades every first grade experience like the breath of life. It is the teacher's indispensable ally in every application of the Waldorf methods.

Dr. Steiner, who evolved this new art of movement, called it "visible speech and tone." It should not, however, be confused with dance art, which is founded upon entirely different premises. Eurythmy is the expression in bodily movement of that inner life and movement of the soul *which precedes utterance through speech or tone.* Indeed, the song or speech of human beings is actually eurythmic movement restricted to the larynx, gesture of the voice instead of gesture of the whole organism. Eurythmy reveals these same gestures by carrying them into bodily expression.

Few modern human beings have the slightest inkling of the lively, mobile character of speech. The more civilized we are the more we repress a tendency to gesticulate while speaking. Indeed, we are so far gone in this repressive tendency that it is fashionable to have dead-pan voices as well as still hands and dead pan faces. Our speech and expressions are stylized to conceal rather than to reveal. Yet, in spite of ourselves every word we speak is a thing of movement, a little dancer dancing out our inmost characteristics.

Individually though our speech is colored, it is built on certain formative principles that are common to people of all nations. A close study of single speech-sounds reveals the fact that a B, an N, a G is as definite a value as blue, white, or vermillion. Every sound is an entirely distinct personality that lives and moves and has its being exactly as does any individual. Its movement is quite typical, no matter what language it is found in. B always shelters and encloses, as in barn, building, box, basket, barrel, bowl, bag, boundary, border, bulwark, bastion, boot, boat, bandage. F has a certain unpredictable suddenness, a swift, light or fierce forward-darting movement, as in flit, flutter, fork, find, fizzle, flick, flicker, fall, fight, fast, forward, fan, fling, flip, fluster, fickle, fancy, fantasy, fairy, feather, fun, fury, frenzy, frantic. G holds its own against opposition, as in go-get, grate, grab, gasp, grasp, grow, groan, goad, gag, grit, gain, grind, grip, grapple, guard. Every other sound, whether vowel or consonant, has its characteristic gesture that may be expressed in movements of our most expressive parts, the hands and arms, supported by movement of the whole body. This gesture is present in every word we speak. Its form is imprinted on the flowing breath-stream with every utterance. The eurythmist, moving to speech, speaks with his whole body, and as he moves he makes visible those inner dynamics out of which speech issues.

Vowels are the tonal element of language, consonants its sculpture. Vowels sing of feelings and emotions. Consonants mold and form, as does the will.

Music too is gesture, and may be translated into eurythmic movement.

To gain a really adequate insight into the whole field of phenomena with which eurythmy is concerned requires many years' study. For this reason eurythmy lessons must be given by specially trained teachers even in the primary grades where the ideal is to have as few special teachers as possible. But all the teachers in Steiner schools need to have some knowledge of eurythmy in order that they may weave its basic principles into the subjects they are teaching.

It will be obvious even from the above incomplete sketch of eurythmy that a profound relationship exists between this art of movement and the teaching of music and the speech arts (writing, reading, story-telling, drama and reciting). Full use is made of this relationship, and its benefits are felt in many ways. It affects the children's grace of movement; it sensitizes hands and fingers; it heightens drawing and modelling ability; it stimulates the musical, poetic and dramatic senses; it relieves strain and tension. Children who do eurythmy speak well and articulate clearly. Even their writing is affected as a result of forming the sounds with plastic movements of the hands and arms. The whole child is roused by eurythmy. It is perhaps the most effective means of strengthening his body and stimulating his artistic capacities.

Eurythmy is also closely interwoven with the teaching of

numbers, with geometry, even with grammar. As far as space allows, the relationship of eurythmy to other subject matter will be concretely illustrated in the following pages.

In the first grade the children learn to experience the difference between round and straight lines as they move on simple curves and geometric patterns. Vowels and consonants are introduced, not from a theoretical standpoint, but rather in the spirit of play to the accompaniment of stories and poems translated into gesture and spatial motion by the teacher and carried out in imitative movement by the children. Various metric and numerical rhythms are practiced. Simple melodies too are translated into tone-eurythmic movement. Rod exercises to promote bodily control and coordination and to develop hand and finger dexterity are emphasized.

The patterns on which the children move together are a prime means of heightening social consciousness. Great pleasure is felt by the children in building up these forms with common timing and similarity of motion. A wealth of such patterns is used to this end.

An important branch of eurythmy is that called curative eurythmy. It lies outside the scope of this volume to attempt description of this highly specialized field. Each school has its curative eurythmist, who works with the school doctor and carries out his prescriptions for those children who need curative exercises of any kind. But there are certain quite general exercises taken from the realm of curative eurythmy that may be done in the morning assembly with all the children. These consist of simple rhythmic motions that have the effect of harmonizing thinking, feeling and will. To the children they are just setting-up exercises of a pleasing nature. But every teacher who has used them regularly knows how helpful they can be in combatting imbalance in his pupils' temperaments.

CHAPTER III

The-Seven-Year-Olds

A good deal of space has necessarily been given to an attempt to indicate the nature of first grade methods and activities, for these form the foundation of all later work. Even so, these indications can scarcely be anything but fragmentary in so short a volume. They are intended rather as direction pointers than as a routine to be rigidly followed. Every teacher will have his own way of meeting the challenge that the nature of children in this phase of development presents to his artistry. Indeed, the only requirement is that he be an artist, or become one.

According to the Waldorf plan the teacher progresses with his pupils from first to second grade; in fact, he continues with them through all eight years of their elementary schooling wherever this is feasible. There are many advantages to such a practice when the teacher is equipped to meet the demands it necessarily makes on his knowledge and ability. If for any reason he cannot meet them, it is of course best that he restrict his work to the first three grades. But these grades form a unity, and no break should therefore occur during the first three years. It is not, as many people believe, an advantage to have young children subjected to a variety of teachers. Such a practice is a prime cause of nervousness and insecurity. The young child needs to know his main teacher as thoroughly and intimately as he knows his parents. He is far more sensitive to change than older children, far more easily strained by the profound readjustments that must be made to new personalities and methods. Primary children are creatures of habit; they want sameness above all else. They want the same story, the same games, the same songs and poems, and they find security in having the same people around them.

There are other advantages in having teachers continue with their pupils. The teacher who in the fourth, fifth or sixth grade can look back on all his pupils' previous learning experiences and build step by step on his own foundations is in a position to endow all his teaching with real unity. His work with the children becomes a living, growing organism for which no one-year stand can ever be a fitting substitute.

To those who might object that no teacher is adequate to such demands, the reply must be that only teachers who can span the entire range of a child's schooling are capable of conceiving any part of it correctly. It is therefore to be hoped that the day is not far distant when these facts will be realized and teachers-in-training will be educated to meet this challenge.

Of course no teacher can be a specialist in every subject. But he is not required to teach any but main lessons, and—in the primary grades—music and handwork. These requirements are by no means too severe. Well-educated persons can meet them easily, and everyone will grant that teachers should be well educated.

Teacher and children, then, progress together from the first to the second grade. They take up their work where they left off for their summer holidays and proceed to build on the foundations laid down in the first grade.

English now becomes a special subject and is assigned its share of main lesson periods. Now as before the spoken word forms the very core of all language experiences. But the fairy tales so dear to the hearts of first graders no longer occupy the center of the stage; their place is taken by legends and animal fables. The fables satisfy the children's deep interest in the animal kingdom, while legends offer them impressions of lofty striving and highlight the noblest human qualities.

The children's need for these more realistic stories reflects their more objective awareness of the world about them. Fairy tales, which a few months before were their native element, are still dearly loved but no longer quite so essential. They are ready now for a sterner form of truth.

The fables and legends that are told and re-told, the poems they learn, the significant impressions that continue to live in them from many different sources now form their writing material. They proceed to learn cursive writing by joining up the printed letters they know from the previous year's work. This flowing script pictures far more truly than printing the movement of the breath as it streams through sound after sound and links them together in smooth continuity.

Grammar, that bugbear of language study, is introduced to second graders for weighty reasons and in a wholly novel way. It is not taught as a set of rules and abstract definitions, but with liveliness and humor. It helps the child penetrate deep into the fascinating mysteries of speech and opens his eyes to the way its structure reflects his own humanness.

Almost any simple story told with a light touch will do as an introduction, provided there is plenty of action in it. The scene may be the Garden of Eden with Adam and Eve gazing wonderingly at the brave new world and naming all the plants and animals. Two children may play these parts while the others enact the parts of the various animals, plants and stones. The children will notice that the stones have to lie stock-still and do nothing, and that the plants are little better off. Plants must stay rooted to the spot; they can only grow taller, send out leaves, blossoms and fragrance, and nod and sway a little in the breeze. But the animals have legs and can move about freely. Some climb trees, some swim, others fly and run and jump, and so on. And Adam and Eve are the freest of all. They can do everything that plants and animals can do, and more besides. They speak; they use their hands to make the most wonderful variety of tools and instruments that serve them in all kinds of ways. The children will have to find many more words to name what people do than they need for animal activities. In this way they receive vivid impressions of the differences between the kingdoms of nature and of man's almost infinite possibilities. They experience the contrast between doing-words, naming-words and describing-words. As they act out the parts of stones, plants, animals and man they find how necessary limbs are to movement. Every time they hear a doing-word their own limbs long to carry out the action. Verbs are the words of will; they are the legs and arms of sentences, setting them in motion. Adjectives, however, stir only the feelings; they speak to the heart. As for nouns, they leave us entirely motionless. We stand apart and look at objects around us, think about them and give them a name. Nouns are the thought words, the heads of sentences.

There are profound social implications in such a study. As the child compares his own possibilities of movement with those of animals he becomes aware of both his superior endowment and his responsibility toward the rest of creation. There is no other creature so free and able as he to take part in the creative world process. He joins his own strength to that of nature and his fellow human beings when he acts, shaping and transforming the world about him. Verbs teach him the responsibility of his human freedom, the joys of creation; they relate him to the world. Nouns separate him from the world in the very act of naming. In his separateness from the world of things he can come to realize how much the world gives him. Let him but name as nouns some of the objects, the foods he needs in daily living and the far places from which they are brought for his enjoyment.

* * * * * *

In arithmetic the children now carry out more complicated operations with the four processes. Imaginative stories still form the basis of these problems. But the children are encouraged to discard their counters as soon as possible and to reckon in their heads. Rhythmic counting accompanied by accented clapping and movement of the whole body is made much of in preparation for learning the multiplication tables. The children learn in this way to count by twos, threes, fours and fives. Once they can do this they begin learning the tables. But in accordance with the principle of wholeness they recite the tables "backwards," naming the product first: e.g., 12 equals 6 times 2.

It will not be long before the discovery is made that certain numbers like 6, 8, 12, 15, 18, 20, 21 and 24 occur in two or more different tables, that certain rhythmic sequences of counting, for example, 2,4,*6*; 8, 10, *12* etc. meet and cross other sequences such as 3,*6*; 9,*12*. These discoveries fill the children with a deep delight in number relationships. Their pleasure can be further heightened by showing them how the same relationships may be expressed in drawings such as a six-pointed star or hexagon made up of two contrastingly colored triangles, illustrating how the two-sequence meets and crosses the three-sequence in their common six, or they can draw a circle with twelve radii in which two halves, three squares, four triangles and six wedges are all contained in one twelveness.

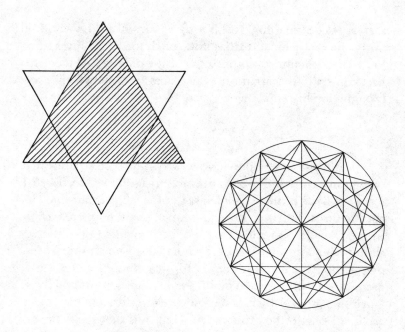

Another illustration of the magic of numbers is a three-drawing which when placed as follows has threeness everywhere:

46

Placed on its tip instead, we see a new number-picture:

★					1
★		★			2
★		★		★	3
★		★			2
★					1

Similar exercises may be carried out with fours and fives or any other number.

Another number puzzle is the following:

$$
\begin{aligned}
1 &= 1, \text{ or } 1 \times 1 \\
1 + 2 + 1 &= 4, \text{ or } 2 \times 2 \\
1 + 2 + 3 + 2 + 1 &= 9, \text{ or } 3 \times 3 \\
1 + 2 + 3 + 4 + 3 + 2 + 1 &= 16, \text{ or } 4 \times 4 \\
1 + 2 + 3 + 4 + 5 + 4 + 3 + 2 + 1 &= 25, \text{ or } 5 \times 5
\end{aligned}
$$

Such interrelationships are everywhere present in the world of numbers. To reveal them is not only to befriend the child with mathematics but to give him impressions of the majesty and harmony of a rhythmically ordered universe that are perhaps the truest kind of mental hygiene.

*   *   *   *   *   *

Painting and modelling are seldom taken as main lesson epochs in the second grade. The nature of the other activities in the curriculum is such as to draw both these arts into constant service. Every main lesson subject involves making an illustrated notebook, for example. Color is never absent from a single lesson, with consequent remarkable records for normal eyesight among children in Steiner schools. Often, however, one handwork period a week is given to painting or modelling in addition to the daily experiences in form and color.

Nature study is continued as before in connection with poetry, legends and imaginative descriptions of natural processes. The earth is always pictured as a living being, which indeed it is. The purpose of these lessons is to enable the child to conceive the world about him truly, yet in that personal, imaginative, living form most natural to his state of consciousness.

Foreign languages continue to be taught as in the first grade. Singing and flute lessons also continue essentially unchanged. Simple ear-training is emphasized and care is taken to give the children a rich experience of tonal beauty both in making and listening to music. The development of the esthetic sense during this phase of childhood prepares the soil for the development of a healthy sense of discrimination in later years.

In handwork, crocheting is introduced, and small projects such as the making of cloth notebook covers are carried out with colorful designs of the children's own creating. In all handwork an important principle is observed: that its products be useful and functional as well as beautiful. The false estheticism that has been our heritage from the Mauve Decade and strewn the civilized world with misnamed "objets d'art" is as anti-social as it is abstract. When the children knit, sew, crochet, weave, spin or do carpentry and bookbinding they must have in mind a concrete use for every object they make, and design it in each least detail to serve its purpose.

Eurythmy lessons in the second grade lead the children into a more conscious forming of vowels and consonants. The tone eurythmy movements for the C major scale are learned, and the children move to simple folk melodies. They also practice the movements for the first five intervals. These studies are an excellent means of enhancing the children's musical awareness and supplement the ear training given in music periods.

Rod exercises, rhythms, and working out the movement of all kinds of geometric patterns are continued. The children learn in eurythmy to carry out in motion the forms they have drawn in their number lessons. This helps greatly to relieve form experiences of their rigid element.

CHAPTER IV

The Eight-Year-Olds

The nature of children in the first and second grades is so similar that there is no essential difference in the curricula of these two years. The third grade, however, represents a transition. The child of eight is leaving one phase of growth behind him and preparing to enter another. Parents and teachers of third graders are apt to say that at this age a child is neither flesh, fowl nor good red herring. Throughout his being there are signs of change not yet accomplished.

The quickened physical growth that takes place during this transition period soon realigns all the child's proportions. His legs and arms seem to lengthen overnight and his whole figure stretches. Yet the face on top of the elongated body still has enough of the baby in it to present a droll contrast to his changed stature.

There is a real drama in this turning point. Past and future states of being are seen wrestling with each other perhaps more clearly than at any other period of childhood. The age of dream is passing, and a new age that will one day culminate in the attainment of full waking consciousness begins to dawn.

The third grade curriculum must keep pace with these events. Again there is no sudden break, but rather a shifting emphasis. The child's need of beauty is as keen as ever; indeed, he is able to experience it far more sensitively than before. But his relation to the world around him changes. He is less caught up in all its processes. He sees the world and its affairs in sharper focus. *And to the extent to which he feels separate from the world he seeks knowledge of it.* From now on his studies will have a more realistic, practical character.

This transition to realism takes place most naturally in the social studies that are now introduced into the curriculum as a main lesson subject. Experiences in this field are an organic continuation and elaboration of those previously gained through nature study. But whereas in the first and second grades the beings and processes of nature were pictured as personalities with thoughts and feelings and impulses, speaking to the child directly or described to him in stories and legends, now they appear in more remote perspective. He learns how the kingdoms of nature mutually support and complete one another in a wonderful harmony of interworking. He visits nearby farms for a concrete experiencing of the dependence of man on plants and animals. It is brought home to him how the earth's rocks and minerals form the very ground he stands on as well as the soil from which plants gain their nourishment. He sees how animals need plants to feed on, and how plants in turn make use of the dung of animals. He learns to know the farm products of his immediate environment. He observes the life of the farm and compares its busy scenes and its varied produce with the simpler picture of an untouched setting where man has not yet broken nature's balance with his spade and plough. Once the surface has been scratched, what infinite pains must be taken to create a new balance, and how richly this improving on nature rewards man's enterprise!

Comparing his home with that of animals whose shelter is in caves, holes and nests, in field and forest, the child becomes aware of the creative abilities with which man has been endowed. He is led to consider what ingenuity has been spent on

51

erecting and beautifying human dwellings. Starting with his own community he studies the building of houses. Perhaps he lives in a modern stone house built of steel and concrete. He learns something of the making of these materials, the drawing up of plans, the building process. He contrasts his home with those of other times and peoples. When his own grandfather's grandfather was a little boy, Indians probably set up their tents at the very spot where he now lives. He contrasts their way of living with his own. In other climates, he learns, other people need homes of quite a different nature. So he comes to study the snow dwellings of the Eskimos in the frigid country to the north of him, the casual shelters of peoples living to the south in steaming jungles. He hears about Arabs in the dry heat of far distant deserts, of the western plains peoples, of the Alpine shepherds whose homes are built high in mountain valleys where great winds would tear the roofs off barns and chalets were they not held in place by heavy boulders.

In these first introductions to social studies all teaching is done through the teacher's spoken word and direct experience gained from making excursions or visiting museums. Descriptions are made as lively and significant as possible. If reference books are needed, the teacher reads them and conveys all the material in his own word-pictures. This keeps the learning process warm and human. It enables the teacher to shape the substance of the subject for the concrete children before him.

* * * * * *

Arithmetic too now begins to center in the children's own practical experiences. But this does not mean setting up a grocery store in the classroom to provide the children with a misnamed "real life situation," or practicing addition by adding up the children's ages. Such procedures are as dreary, as abstract, as barren of warm personal interest as any resorted to in old-fashioned textbooks. There is no living Methuselah whose hoary years correspond to the sum of the children's ages. Nor is it normal to do one's shopping in a schoolroom. Far better take the children outside the school to buy some essential equipment if no real life situations involving numbers can be found inside it! But there is certain to be a wealth of such opportunites in every human group. Sheila, for example, has a baby brother just three months old, which makes her at eight and a half thirty-four times the baby's age. But the baby seems to be catching up fast, for on Sheila's next birthday she will be only twelve times as old as he. Or Johnny, who is earning a ten-cent weekly salary by walking the neighbor's dog, is saving to buy roller skates. He has already worked ten weeks. How much longer will he have to wait to buy the skates, which cost three dollars? Such matters are real, for Sheila is devoted to the baby and some of her friends have been allowed to see and play with him, and Johnny's heart hangs on those skates. Most of his friends already have some and are waiting almost as eagerly as he for the time to come when he can skate with them. Examples like these involve the children's feelings, not just their heads. There are other immediate needs such as measuring cloth for handwork projects in which the children are deeply interested. Any community is bound to have hosts of practical number problems.

Rhythmic reciting and stepping out the tables is continued. At this age the children take pleasure in the mental gymnastics involved in puzzles like "take six, add twelve, subtract nine, divide by three," and so on, and the wealth of number harmonies to be discovered in a form such as that below (see page 55) will awe them for days, perhaps for a life, as indeed it may. They find all their rhythmic experiences pictured in it. The rows of numbers proceed in an astonishing variety of orderly progressions. The numbers at the top of the figure progress from ten to thirty by ever smaller leaps: 8,6,4,2. Its neighbors on both sides take still shorter jumps, this time with odd numbers: 7,5,3,1. The next on each side take still shorter steps: 6,4,2; and so on. Who ever said numbers were dull or abstract or meaningless when before one's very eyes they grow into lovely forms like the lily pads floating in the schoolroom frog-pond!

* * * * * *

Just as in the first grade, fairy tales were the *pièce de résistance* of the English lessons, in the second grade, fables and legends, so the third grade, too, has its treasury of stories of a kind peculiarly suited to the eight-year-old: the stories and poetry of the Old Testament. These stories, in that they deal largely with real persons and happenings, are the children's first introduction to history. How potently they picture man's awakening with Adam, his plunge from Paradise into earthly struggle, his strength, his courage to endure, his growth through effort! These dramatic scenes closely parallel the eight-year-old's own experience. They touch him where he lives, and the glorious language in which they are clothed has a vitality akin to his.

A brilliantly illustrated book soon emerges from the Old Testament drama and the stories are re-told there in the child's own words. Powerful psalms are added to the pages of his poetry notebook.

His grammar studies continue. When he writes a sentence he puts the doing-words down in red, the most active of colors. Blue, cool and withdrawing, best expresses the nature of nouns. Adjectives, like feelings, may be as many-colored as the rainbow.

Spelling now receives a good deal of attention, for this subject has social implications of great import. From the first the children have been told that words are written as they are "because people write them this way." This is not to say that

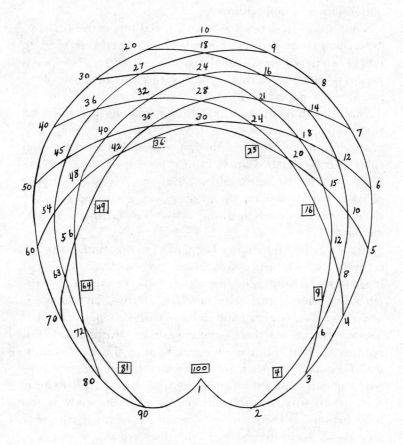

changes may not be desirable, but if they are made, it will be for objective reasons acceptable to everyone. In the meantime, there must be a reasonable unanimity in written symbols, and to respect this necessity does much to engender a sense of social obligation in young children.

Some phonetic work has been carried on in the first two grades and is continued as needed. The children keep spelling notebooks in which mis-spelled words are entered. No special period is set aside for this work. It forms a natural part of the main lesson period in English.

Painting, drawing and modelling continue in connection with all main lessons rather than as separate periods. It is misleading to give children the impression that art is a special subject to be pursued apart from other experiences. In later years certain technical problems of art may be made the object of special study, but in the lower grades color and form are interwoven into every learning activity as indispensable elements.

In music the children now begin to learn notation. Flutes are accordingly no longer played by copying the teacher's fingering, but by learning how finger positions correspond to written notes. Simple one-voice melodies are read and sung.

Tone eurythmy goes hand in hand with these musical studies. Movements for the C major scale are learned and then applied in short folk melodies. Study of the intervals continues. There is further practice in listening to intervals and melodic sequences and then translating what is heard into gesture.

In speech eurythmy the children go on to the study of gestures expressing the many-colored moods of poetry. By now they are so fluent in movement that they are able to work out poems with a smooth flow of gesture and appropriate expression. Exercises in expansion and contraction, in joy and sorrow, in lightness and heaviness prepare the children for a more conscious experiencing of self hood. Other exercises are used to strengthen the will, to develop social feeling, and to heighten intelligence. It is quite possible to do this through movement. As the child *moves* so he *is*. Eurythmy, in developing ease, strength, and skill of movement, is a potent factor in developing the whole child and awaking and bringing out the finest capacities he possesses.

In handwork, simple sewing is introduced, and caps, mufflers, sweaters, or other useful articles are crocheted and knitted. Boys learn these skills for the same developmental reasons as the girls and in order that they may become every bit as self-sufficing and efficient. After the first conventional masculine protest they simply love it.

Physical education makes its first appearance in the third grade curriculum. In the two previous years eurythmy and free play supplied the children's need of bodily activity. Now a turning point has been reached in their development; the spirit now lays a firmer hold upon the body. This is reflected in the children's more awakened, self-conscious state of being. Physical education has the task of helping this development. The children are given a variety of gymnasium and playground apparatus and encouraged to engage in all kinds of big muscular activities under the teacher's supervision. Story-plays in rhythmic verses embodying vigorous motions such as sawing, hammering, chopping, etc., are enacted by the children. The teacher always does the reciting of these verses, for it is important that the children's activity be undivided. There is a close relationship between speech and the motion of the hands and arms, as may be observed in the tendency to gesticulate when we speak. Strenuous movement of the hands and arms, both in physical education and eurythmy, absorbs all the energy of the moving person, and attempts to use the voice at such a time are injurious to the child's whole being.

Foreign languages continue to be taught in the first two grades. But whereas formerly the children simply spoke in imitation of their teachers, learning stories, games and poems by heart, now they begin to learn the foreign language names of single objects in their surroundings. The English word, however, is never interposed between the object and its foreign name, for to do so is to make speaking another language mere translation.

* * * * * *

From the above all too sparse indications of the nature of these first three years of schooling it may be apparent in what sense the educational system described here strives to be as organic as the child's growth itself. There is nothing of the haphazard or perfunctory about it. Its least detail is shaped in accordance with the needs of the phase of development through which the child is passing. Each such detail is an organic part of the whole curriculum.

The curriculum in turn is conceived as a means of supporting the whole child's growth, but to serve this growth we must know what the whole child is and how he develops. This is the crux of the educator's problem. Adults no longer remember their own state of being during early childhood and few are able to observe children with sufficient keenness to gain a really searching insight into a consciousness so different from their own; the education to which most of us were subjected has done little to sensitize us to the phenomena of other individuals' inmost experience. Moreover, we habitually conceive of children as sharing our own state of being. As Harwood points out in his *The Way of A Child*, "The reason why we are in such a hurry today to make children little intellectuals is perhaps that we can hardly conceive of any other form of consciousness." Actually, the child sees the world in a wholly different way. Rudolf Steiner's remarkable ability to observe psychological phenomena enabled him to discover the significant fact that until shortly before puberty the child's consciousness normally has a pictorial rather than a conceptual character. He founded his elementary school methods on this basic recognition. Comparing his methods with those of educators whose appeal was directed chiefly to the child's conceptual powers, Dr. Steiner once asked, "I wonder what you would say if you were to see someone with a plate of fish before him carefully cutting away the flesh and eating the bones? You would certainly be afraid the bones might choke him and that in any case he would not be able to digest them. On another level, the level of the soul, exactly the same thing happens when we give the child dry, abstract ideas instead of living pictures, instead of something that engages the activity of his whole being."

The child's whole being is called into play by an artistic education such as that conceived by Dr. Steiner, for art speaks to the whole human being, not just to his thinking. Art fires the will and harnesses its strength through the objective discipline that each artistic medium imposes on the artist. Art profoundly engages the feelings. It develops that capacity for inward picturing out of which at a later age thought is born.

Every art is centered, no matter how subtly, in the rhythmic element. During the child's elementary schooling when he is essentially a rhythmic being, art is therefore his natural province. How wholesomely the rhythmic nature of his learning maintains him in bodily well-being! The head tires when appealed to for too long a period; the legs and arms are exhausted by prolonged motor effort. But the child's rhythmic organs know nothing of tiring. His heart beats steadily throughout a lifetime; his lungs fill and empty effortlessly. It is easy to see that an education everywhere permeated with the rhythmic element is one that least tires the learner and best promotes healthy development.

The elementary schoolchild's need of living pictures requires the teacher to become an artist at knowledge. He must be able to discover the life and movement, the color, the magic, the warm human interest in every phase of reality he offers his pupils. He must be as sensitive as a musician in listening to the tone of his class and allowing it to teach him his procedures. He must know many secrets of human nature and development. He must avoid pedantry like poison, never entering into dry literal explanations or pressing meanings. To give the children answers that hint at things they will not fully understand until several years later is to give them knowledge to grow on rather than mere information.

In the first three grades stories are the teacher's chief means of making learning live. Fairy tales and legends do not lead the child away from reality, quite the contrary; they lead him toward it by means of living picture-symbols charged with profoundest meaning. A child deprived of fairy stories grows up poor and stunted in his inner life, for he has lacked essential nourishment.

The teacher who uses the Steiner curriculum is not restricted to any set procedure. He is completely free to shape his lessons as he himself thinks best. But there is a fundamental unity in the work of groups of teachers using this approach, a unity that comes from the deep reverence in which they hold the divine in man and universe.

CHAPTER V

The Nine-Year-Olds

By nine most of the changelings of the previous year have accomplished their change and reappear in school after the summer holidays with a strangely different look and new reserve. It is a sad day for them and their teacher if he cannot become a new person with them and win their trust afresh by revealing strengths they have not known in him before. For their new selfhood sits insecurely in the saddle, filling them with a deep sense of uneasiness. Now, more than ever, they have need of adults whose character and talents make them feel how fine it is to be a human being. To have such a teacher throws light on the path ahead. They need this illumination, for the rosy glow of early childhood that made the world so magically bright is gone forever.

Inner and outer worlds are no longer one world for the nine-year-old. They have been irrevocably sundered. The greatest care must now be taken to bring the outer world to the child in a way that everywhere discovers its human meaning.

No study is as ideally fitted to offer strength and comfort to the child at this critical moment as the study of man himself. It begins with a contemplation of man's upright stature. Man alone, of all the myriad creatures in the universe, is able to wrest his head free of the hold of gravity and stand erect. He moves over the earth in perfect balance. How different he looks

61

from the animals with their horizontal spines and their heads dangling almost to the ground!

Man's hands, too, are free. They need not serve him solely as humble carriers like an animal's forepaws, but can be used to perform the most varied and wonderful functions.

Man has another great gift, the gift of speech. Animals cannot tell us what goes on inside them. We can only guess at their feelings when they bark or mew or grunt or roar or whinny. But human beings are able to pour all their thoughts, desires and feelings into words that tell us about them.

To have a really vivid experience of the contrast between man and animal, teacher and children can get down on all fours and find out how it feels to be in the position of a dog, a cat, a pig, a cow, a horse or any other familiar creature, to have one's head down near the earth, one's nose sniffing and rooting, one's mouth biting, gnawing, tearing, one's voice so inarticulate, one's hands and arms mere feet and legs. When one disengages oneself from the animal position, how lofty the head seems, how large and cool its perspective! Somewhere deep within him the child understands what makes man a thinker. Regaining the use of his hands he knows what makes man a creator and an artist. In hands and head he experiences his capacity for human freedom.

When he looks at the human form again the child sees it with a different consciousness. He sees how still the head is compared with the animal's. It sits motionless on the shoulders and is carried about like a man on horseback. The head is an aristocratic lazy-bones. It leaves practical work to other members of the body. The legs and arms are the real workers. Our legs carry us where we need to go, but they can only serve their owner; they can never be lent to work for others as the hands may be. Hands can do deeds of love. With their hands men become the servants of man and nature.

Animals use their heads as men use their hands, to thrust

and pull, to lift and carry. The human head performs none of these functions. It sits aloft like a sentinel keeping watch and receiving impressions. Whereas in animals the head continually reaches out into the environment, in man its stillness and the lofty seclusion of its position actually signify a withdrawal from the world.

The human form has a wonderful harmony. No part is overemphasized at the expense of another. This is not true of animals. The elephant, the giraffe, the monkey all exhibit structural distortions in keeping with the world about them. They are one with their environment; they complete and reflect their natural surroundings. But man is in a different category. He is everywhere a stranger to the earth and at the same time at home in every part of it. He preserves his form essentially intact no matter what environmental influence is brought to bear upon him.

The head and limbs of man are in striking contrast. The head is formed on the principle of roundness; it is almost a perfect sphere. Inside is the soft brain-mass, outside a bony covering as hard as rock. The limbs are built on just the opposite principle; they are straight and linear, and the bone is here inner support rather than outer covering. The chest structure combines something of both the round and linear principles.

The head tends toward stillness, the limbs toward motion. The chest in between alternately dilates and rests in a rhythmic pulsing that wrests life itself from an active balancing of two extremes.

The threefold human organism—head, chest and limbs— thus becomes a study in both form and movement. Children who have had several years of modelling and eurythmy are prepared to enter into such a study with a capacity to experience these realities vividly.

Once they have grasped the threefold structure of the human

form, the children's attention may be called to the fact that each separate part of the body is built on the same threefold pattern. One can begin with the head; it is really a "head" only in its domelike upper part; only there is it really round and without movement, for the breathing organs of the head form a kind of dilating chest in the middle portion, and the limbs of the head are the mobile jaws.

The legs and arms, too, embody the same three structures, exhibiting the round, immobile head-principle in the knobs inserted into hip and shoulder joints, the chest-principle in the flexibility and semi-freedom of the knee and elbow, and the limbs-proper in the agile feet and hands.

The hands and feet in their turn carry out the same motives. The heel at the one extreme is round and rigid, the arch flexible and curving, the toes and fingers linear and highly mobile. The children will make thrilling discoveries of this kind as they look for the head, chest and limbs in the various parts of the body, and they will find them even in so small a part of the organism as a single finger.

When they again compare the human form with that of various animals, their respect for man is heightened by finding that in man alone have these three basic structural principles been harmonized and carried through to ultimate perfection. There is not a single animal whose head, for example, has attained real roundness, whose foot has all three principles embodied in heel, arch and toes. The ape, man's nearest relative among the animals, makes an excellent object of comparison. Studying his head form with its crushed, sloping forehead, its heavy thrusting jaw, its fearful fangs, its flattened nose—observing its stooping posture, its dangling upper limbs that are more like legs than arms, its strange hand, its flat-foot, the children see how great is the difference between this brute beast, which has fallen so pathetically short of humanness, and man. A visit to the zoo to have a good look at him makes a tremendous impression on them. When, back in the school-room, they try to get under his skin in a faithful impersonation of his posture, his gait, his expression, his voice, they will realize as they never could through words how far removed man is from that specialized distortion that each animal form betrays.

A study of the forms of various animals will make this principle of specialization still more clear. The horse's life in his environment has distorted the foot form almost beyond recognition. The horse's toes have disappeared and been replaced by a horny hoof. His heel is actually half way up his leg! Studying the cow one sees that this animal has specialized in the direction of becoming all metabolism. One stomach is not enough to suit the cow! She must have three! And the heavy head that looks so difficult to lift is more an extension of the cow's long digestive tract than a perceptive organism as in man.

Some creatures present especially striking examples of this specializing tendency in the animal form. One may point out the kangaroo, which is a specialist in locomotion and has tremendously developed lower limbs. Bivalves, on the other hand, have no limbs at all and are scarcely more than primitive heads with a soft mass inside a hard outer covering. Fishes represent a specialized chest development. They are all spine and ribs and breathing organism. Such specialization in one of the three systems always takes place at the expense of a stunting of the other parts. Man's capacity to refrain from specialization has preserved him from this stunting, and we therefore see in him a beauty, a perfection and a harmony of form that no animal can equal.

A contrasting of the human hand with the paws of animals serves more than any other study to bring out the fact of the non-specialization of the human form. Yet this hand that is so little fitted for climbing, tearing and digging is sensitive and intelligent. It can make tools that enable man to do everything animals do and to go far beyond them in performing specialized functions.

In all these studies man and animal are contemplated only in their external forms; no investigations of their structure are pursued below the skin. Children of nine have not yet developed to the point where they can look without horror at the denuded bones and inner organs.

The study of man and animal offers rich opportunity for the telling of stories and legends, the learning of poems, the painting and drawing of pictures, and modelling plays an especially important role. Now for the first time the child is concerned with detail and exactness of form. In the first three grades his modelling activity had an entirely different character. He created wholes, not parts. He made Christmas scenes complete with Joseph, Mary, the Child, the shepherds and Magi, the ox and ass. Or perhaps he modelled a scene from a fairy tale or legend, with not a character missing. But now he models the heads of man and the animals he is studying. As his fingers shape the sphere of wax or clay into the rounded head of man and then transform it into that of some animal, he can experience in still another way what forces have been at work to create these differences.

Such a study is an important contribution to the child's social training. To come to know man in concrete detail as the crown of creation is to inspire the deepest reverence for human beings. To have a vivid experience of the animal's brute limitations is to rouse pity and a sense of man's responsibility toward this lower kingdom.

* * * * * *

Fourth grade English is also designed to give the child support at this critical phase of development. This is the age of hero worship when he is consciously seeking an inspiring picture of human nature and a model on whom he may deliberately pattern his behavior. Sagas, therefore, now provide him with ideal reading and story-telling material, particularly those of Irish, Icelandic and Scandinavian origin, with their characteristic stress on strength and boldness rather than on cunning. Sagas in poetic form are especially well-liked at this age. But there should be plenty of contrast in both poetry and reading, for the nine-year-old has broken away from the primary child's love of sameness and requires as much variety as possible to enrich and develop his intensified inner life.

Composition still confines itself to simple narration of the child's own real experiences. But children of this age are beginning to become highly sensitive to the beauty of language. Words have more meaning, a richer qualitative content than they had before. They reveal more of human nature. This is therefore an ideal time to help them cultivate beauty and good style in writing.

Grammar studies continue, always from the standpoint of discovering the human being in the forms of speech. Nouns, for example, are the sculptors and architects of sentences, adjectives the painters, verbs the dramatists and actors. The relation of a preposition to its noun is a human gesture. Grammar so studied helps to provide a valuable support for the child's developing ego. It relates to his daily experiences; its rules are the laws of his own nature and activity. To discover them is to be steadied by finding himself more fully.

Letter forms are also introduced in the fourth grade main lessons in English. In letter writing the child enters as an independent self into formal communication with other selves, perhaps even with unfamiliar ones to whom he writes for some practical business reason. Any previous concern with letters would have had little meaning for a child who had not yet felt some degree of isolation from the world and a consequent need to bridge it. Now it helps to relate him to the world in a new way and signifies a real enlargement of his horizon.

* * * * * *

Fourth grade arithmetic introduces fractions and decimals. The children are fascinated to discover that the bigger the number in the denominator the smaller the fraction, that one sixteenth is smaller than one half, one quarter and one eighth. All kinds of concrete objects like the apples and oranges that are to be the children's recess snacks may be used to demonstrate these truths. To have a visual experience of mathematical facts before forming mental concepts about them is to give the thought process ground to stand upon.

Fractions may also be taught through movement. For example, two children may stand at a given distance from each other. The space between them is then bisected by a third child, the half-space again bisected by a fourth, and so on, each child naming the fraction created by his motion. This exercise can be carried out with thirds, fifths, and so on. Once the children have grasped the principle in spatial movement, it can be transferred to paper.

The child's previous experience of the interrelationships of number families has prepared them to grasp the principle of adding and subtracting in terms of common denominators.

* * * * * *

Social studies claim an extended series of fourth grade main lesson periods.

The child of nine, if he has developed normally, has not yet formed clear concepts of space and time. He knows only the familiar space he himself has lived in, the familiar time he has spent living. Unless he has travelled widely he can hardly imagine the world beyond his own immediate horizon. It is a myth, fascinating to hear about, but quite unreal. It will be useless for the teacher to prepare him for geography by picturing the earth as a huge ball whirling in cosmic space. The child cannot abstract himself from the earth sufficiently to form such an external concept of it. Such a picture only confuses him. Is the ground he stands on not obviously flat and motionless?

Earlier ages of man are also beyond his real comprehension. He can only picture past time in terms of the experience of real, living, breathing people like his parents and grandparents. Even so it moves him strangely to hear about things that happened to them long before he was born.

For these fourth graders social studies begin with the familiar things of the child's own time and environment and lead him gradually to an experience of less familiar places and events.

It is good at the outset to give the child a picture of the relation of the place he lives in to the "points of the compass" and the general configuration of the landscape. Let him point out where the sun rises and sets, in what direction the cold north and the warm south lie. If he is a New Yorker he lives on an island with great land masses stretching to the west of him and a vast ocean lying to the east. He lives in the world's largest city. Ships go in and out of its harbor, connecting it with lands far beyond the sea, and many bridges span the rivers that separate it from the mainland. Over them in both directions pours a constant stream of cars, trains and trucks carrying the things people need and have produced for each other. The shops and markets are full of produce that has come from distant places, and the factories are busy making things to send away. The children will want to go about and see them, to watch the ships, to climb some of the tall buildings, to cross the bridges, to have a boat-ride around the island and see it from every angle. How imposing it looks with its glittering towers, its broad avenues, its soaring bridges!

One can then try to imagine how this island looked before the white men came and transformed it. It had the same shape; the same rivers girdled it, but no bridges spanned them then. The only ships to be seen were the small dugouts and birch-bark canoes of the Indians. Where not a tree grows, there were deep forests. Where traffic roars there was stillness broken only by bird-calls and the wind's song. For the Indians who lived on Manhattan moved through the forest so lightly that not a twig snapped under their moccasins.

All that was long, long ago. But the island looked different even when Joan's father was a little boy. There were only two short bridges then, one skyscraper, and not a single tunnel had been dug under the rivers. When Joan's father's father was a boy it looked still more different. There were no automobiles, no bridges, no tall buildings. Life moved at a slow pace. New York was like a country village then, and there were forests and meadows uptown where people went picnicing and had farms and summer houses.

By the time the class gets back to Joan's great-grandfather there are three ancestors standing in line. By the time it gets back to the Indians at least ten children are needed to form a link of people with the past, each one representing a real generation that once actually lived and breathed. Perhaps each such generation brought forth a famous man or two whose life-story must be told for local and temporal coloring. With what shattering effect the life of each successive generation was changed by some new invention or discovery—events that changed the face of the city no less than the faces of the people who made their homes in it!

Picture maps may be drawn of New York and its surroundings at different periods, showing the actual colors of the land changing with the city's growth and the unchanging blue of

70

the rivers and the ocean: first the unbroken green of primeval forests, then the Dutch village at the tip of the island, then the big brick and brownstone town, and finally the overwhelming flood of gray and silver modernity dotted with a few green parks. The hills, the trees, the farms and meadows with their human and animal populations may all be indicated in pictorial fashion.

Telling the story of Manhattan or of any other human community inevitably leads to a study of the geography and history of a wider region with which its life is closely interwoven. In the case of a world capital like New York it is difficult to keep from following threads all too far afield. The teacher will have to exercise real restraint not to exceed the bounds fixed by the nature of the nine-year-old's consciousness. This problem is perhaps best solved by giving the children a selection of vivid pictures and contrasting impressions rather than minute, logically progressing geographical and historical analyses.

* * * * * *

The study of two foreign languages continues in the fourth grade. But the children's understanding of grammar has progressed to a point that enables them consciously to grasp the rules underlying the construction of these languages. They begin to write as well as to speak them.

In music the child's newly strengthened individuality now gives him the ability to hold his own in part-singing as he could not have done successfully before. Canons and rounds form a natural bridge to this exciting new skill. He shows his first real delight in harmony. There is a profound satisfaction to be experienced in the sound of intermingling voices mutually completing and supporting one another. Although he would not so define it, he is having a foretaste of the free, creative brotherhood of man. Such experiences go far to gentle

71

the combative spirit that also awakens in him with this phase of development.

The minor mode, which in its melancholy inwardness formerly depressed his childish gayety, now answers a deep-felt need. It leads him into himself on an adventure of self-discovery. Major leads him out again into wholesome brightness. How he loves the contrast between these two modes, between slow and fast, high and low, soft and loud!

His study of notation continues. This is the age when he becomes capable of real skill and musicianship, and he should be given full opportunity to develop it.

Tone eurythmy as always goes hand in hand with his other musical experiences. He learns the eurythmic representation of several new major scales and carries polyphonic compositions into movement that expresses their rhythmic, melodic and harmonic elements.

Speech eurythmy in the fourth grade concerns itself intensively with grammar. Active and passive verbs, nouns, adjectives and all the subtle expressiveness of speech such as is embodied in question and answer, exclamation, direct and indirect quotation—in other words, in punctuation—is translated into appropriate gesture. Rod and form exercises are continued. A special emphasis is given to exercises that stimulate social feeling.

Handwork periods are given largely to sewing. The children are taught the various seams and stitches and their application. Each child makes himself some article of clothing.

Physical education continues essentially unchanged. Here as in the third grade two short weekly periods are assigned to this activity.

CHAPTER VI

The Ten-Year-Olds

A year's growth often works revolutionary changes in children of elementary school age, but teachers seldom find it difficult to recognize the fifth grader for the child they knew in fourth grade. His horizon has widened considerably; he has become steadier and more self-confident. But he has not usually undergone any basic transformation. He has simply enhanced his recent gains in consciousness and grown more accustomed to being an isolated self, seeing the world in a new perspective.

Like the third grader, however, he is about to leave another phase of childhood behind him and to cross a new threshold of experience. The curriculum of this year must, therefore, not only continue to build on already established foundations but introduce certain new elements in order to prepare him properly for his next step forward.

History is one such new element. In the lower grades there has been no essential difference between history and story. The children learned something of the lives and times of great personages—Old Testament characters, Norse and Irish heroes, and personalities who figured in the study of their own homeland. History had a personal and pictorial nature. No attempt was made to introduce exact temporal concepts or to proceed in strict sequences. Now, however, history becomes a special main lesson subject, as does geography. These two subjects are not treated together until two years later, for to do so would mean losing the benefits of both for the child's sound development at this critical moment. History, telling as it does the story of man's deeds and strivings, stirs the child to a more intense experiencing of his own humanness; he lives in the drama of history as though he himself were involved in every happening. As he studies the dynamic progress of humanity through many different phases of consciousness he is led to see himself and the age he lives in as the heirs of an evolutionary process that he in turn will help carry forward. History moves from the unfamiliar past to the familiar present, from the impersonal to the personal. *History brings the child to himself.* Geography does exactly the opposite: *it leads him away from himself out into ever wider spaces*, from the familiar to the unfamiliar. It stretches his consciousness to include all the peoples of the earth. In this sense the two studies move in opposite directions, supplementing each other by their very difference.

History accordingly starts in the fifth grade with times so hoary as to be almost mythical: with the childhood of civilized humanity in ancient India as we know it from the remnants of poetry that have come down to us from the final stages of that first great culture. The ancient Indians were dreamers, men so different from ourselves that we can hardly imagine their state of consciousness. The earth seemed to them a place of toil and darkness from which they longed with all their hearts to be released. They lived in a warm and fertile country, but even so the slight effort necessary to maintain their lives seemed painful. The ancient Indians were a deeply religious people; there were many wisemen among them to whom they looked up with great reverence.

The ancient Persian culture that followed the Indian had a different character. The Persians, too, regarded the earth as the

74

kingdom of darkness, but they were a far more active people than the Indians. They felt an impulse to transform the earth, and so they learned to till the soil, to domesticate animals and to make use of all the earth's goodness to enrich their lives. The Persians were sun worshippers. They believed that they were helping the sun-god conquer the spirit of darkness in the earth as they went about their work transforming it and making it yield up its riches.

The next great culture was that of the Chaldeans, the Hebrews, the Assyrians, the Babylonians and the Egyptians. The Egyptians came to love the earth and their earthly possessions so much that they were loath to leave them at death. They caused their bodies to be mummified and buried in the earth's rocky caverns surrounded by all their treasures.

Next comes the civilization of the Greeks, with whom ancient history ends. Wonderful pictures can be developed of this culture that so richly deserved the title of the Golden Age. It was a time in which men spent their fullest powers to make earth-life beautiful. The Greeks loved the earth more than any other people. They felt thoroughly at home in their sunny islands.

Like the Persians and the Egyptians before them, the Greeks were sun worshippers, though all three peoples called the sun-god by different names. Some of the glorious poetry that sprang from this sun worship is learned and compared.

Every means is used to give the children a vivid impression of these four ancient cultures. They read translations of Indian, Persian, Egyptian and Hebrew and Greek literature and wherever possible learn a short poem in Sanskrit, Hebrew and Greek. They study the hieroglyphic symbols of the Egyptians. They see samples of the arts and crafts of the various ancient peoples and try their hands at creating in a similar fashion.

History in the fifth grade thus becomes a pictorial-artistic study of the evolution of human consciousness. It is an education of the children's feeling rather than of their memory for facts and figures, for it requires inner mobility to enter sympathetically into these ancient states of being so different from their own.

* * * * * *

Geography, which in the fourth grade acquainted the child more closely with his own community and its immediate surroundings, now leads him much farther afield. The element of contrast should be emphasized in this as in all fourth and fifth grade studies. In a land as full of cultural, climatic and geographical variety as our own it is not difficult to proceed in a colorful fashion.

The study of American geography has tremendously dramatic possibilities that should be fully exploited. Vivid word-pictures may be painted of the various stages of the white man's struggle with the wilderness and of its effect upon his character and culture. The life of the stern Puritan working the rocky soil of his cold northern homeland may be contrasted with that of the southern aristocrat on his fertile acres that burgeoned almost without effort on his part, or with the life of the adventurous settlers of the Ohio Valley and the great western plains. The same differences are brought home to the children in another way as they sing the restrained music of the northerners, the southerners' rollicking or sentimental ditties, the Kentucky mountain folk-tunes, the negro spirituals, the nostalgic, subtly accented songs of the cowboys. They dance the dances, study the costumes, the manners, the legends, the architecture, the crafts, even the cookery of the various regions. Every consideration of the earth's physical features is linked up with a study of the way human life has been lived in the region, the human uses made of natural resources, the industry and produce, and the means of exchange between each such region and the rest of the country.

Relief maps and picture maps are made, and the tidal rolling back of the frontier by the various national groups is indicated in different colors.

Every study taught in Steiner schools is a social study, but geography serves more than any other as a unifier of the children's learning experiences. It is the cement that holds the curriculum together. For this reason it is often taken as the final main lesson subject and closely related to details of the studies that have preceded it in the year's program.

* * * * * *

The study of man and animal is continued in the fifth grade. During this year, the children are given a more complete picture of the animal kingdom. They go to the country, the zoo, the aquarium to become acquainted with less familiar species than those studied in the fourth grade. The specialization of a great variety of animal forms is observed in detail. The giraffe, for example, presents an extraordinary picture of over-emphasized neck development. Its whole body is fixed in a gesture of craning. The kangaroo is in many ways its opposite pole; it goes about provided with a camp-chair in the form of a heavy tail which it uses as a support in sitting. Whereas the whole giraffe has gone up into its neck, the whole kangaroo has gone down into its hind part. The giraffe's spindly legs hardly look as though they were meant to carry it; the kangaroo's hind legs are mightily developed, though its forelegs are grotesquely stunted. In the tapir and the elephant the upper lip and the nose have grown together and become one elongated organ. The squid or cuttlefish is a tongue-organism, the jelly-fish a brain floating around without its skull. The snail is a two-legged creeper with its stomach hung over its shoulder in a bag. The mouse is a trunk on four insignificant legs; it has sharp teeth which keep on growing like our finger and toe-nails and compel it to gnaw continually. The bat, which has no legs at all, has a set of claws on the end of its wings instead.

Grotesque though their forms are, the animals are all distinguished by some special gift not possessed by man. The eagle has keener vision than any other creature. It can look down and see a rabbit or a chicken on the ground a mile below. The monkey, the squirrel, the leopard are sure climbers, as much at home in the treetops as on solid earth. They do not grow dizzy at great heights and fall as man would. The dog has an acute sense of smell. The deer, the moose, the horse are swift runners. Each animal is found to have its special ability.

Man has none of these abilities by nature, for he has re-frained from specializing. But this very non-specialization makes him free in a sense that the animal can never be. His behavior cannot be predicted from his shape and equipment. The same evolution which has withheld him from special-ization and given him the potentiality of freedom has also endowed him with the power of thought. Through exercising thought he has invented means whereby he flies more swiftly than the bird, swims under water, ascends great heights safely, and looks thousands of miles out into space, which the eagle's keen eye can never penetrate. He travels in his trains, cars and airplanes faster than any of nature's runners, and he uses his hands and his voice to become an artist and to create beauty.

The child's attention may be drawn to the fact that every animal species over-emphasizes some one of the three systems that in man have been held in perfect balance. The lower ani-mals are one-sided head-developments in both form and func-tion; the fish, chest organisms; the higher mammals, limb and digestive systems.

After this survey of man and animal the children will under-

78

stand in what sense man may be called the whole animal kingdom resolved into a single perfect form—the animal kingdom being a fanwise projection of specialized fragments of the human being.

* * * * *

Having come to know something of man and the kingdom of nature closest to him, the children now proceed to a study of the plant world. This means studying the earth as a living organism, for the plant is only to be grasped in relation to the earth, just as the animal is only to be grasped in relation to the human being. A plant torn out of its natural setting at once becomes strangely unreal, as unreal as a hair or a finger nail isolated from the person they grew on. Goldenrod is unthinkable apart from an autumnal meadow, violets from a spring woodland. When the teacher speaks of plants, he therefore speaks of the whole earth organism as the living body from which they sprouted.

Only the root of the plant belongs wholly to the earth. In its root the plant is an earth-dweller imprisoned in darkness, but in its blossom it is a creation of the warm sunlight. The plant comes into being between earth and sky. It is most truly plant-like in its green middle portion, stalk and leaves. Its blossom is a visitor from far beyond the earth, while its root, like Proserpine, has become a hostage.

The plant form is a study in the subtlest movement. The root is built on the principle of contraction like the mineral element in which it makes its home. The blossom rays out its petals like the sun. The stalk and leaves in between alternately expand and contract, often in the movement of an ascending spiral. When the plant matures, its expansion into the blossom is inhibited, and the seed is formed in a final contracting motion.

79

How prodigal earth and sun have been in plant creation! Even a tiny portion of the earth's surface shows us a greater variety of forms and colors than the eye can grasp. How it changes in the different seasons! The spot we visited in April has been transformed by June and once again by September. A wave of white and pale yellow blossoming follows close upon the sun's climb toward a vertical position in the spring time. Lush, saturated greens, rich reds, roses, blues and purples accompany the glorious floodtide of the summer's warmth. At the first hint of autumn, when the sun's rays fall slanting on the earth, come the mauves, the old golds like a concentrated heritage of summer sunshine.

Studying some of the familiar plants of his own environment the child can observe how differently earthly and cosmic forces work together in the variety of plant forms. There is the buttercup with a slender thread of stalk, feathery leaves and an open chalice drinking in the sunlight in an unshaded meadow; the violet, hidden by its great leaves and seeking out the cool, moist, shadowed places. Some plants, like the poppy and the sweet pea, have become all blossom; some, like the radish, beet and carrot, all root; others, like the potato, which masquerades as a root, are really stalks demeaning themselves by creeping underneath the ground. The stinging nettle, instead of using the warmth element to bring forth a brightly colored blossom, draws the fire of the summer sun into its leafage and burns unwary passers-by!

After discovering some of the secrets of the plant life found in his own environment the child's attention is drawn to vegetation in other parts of the earth. Taking an imaginary journey overland toward the north pole he finds the vegetation gradually dwindling in height and spreading itself out horizontally instead. Blossoms and leaves grow smaller; the stalk is shortened. The root parts, on the other hand, become enormously enlarged and thickened. Here we see earth forces gaining the upper hand over the cosmic force of warmth and sunlight. The farther north one goes the more pronounced is this tendency. The last plants to be found are the ground-clinging mosses and lichens. Then vegetation ceases altogether.

An imaginary journey toward the equator presents a picture of diametrically opposite conditions. The farther south one travels from the temperate zone the more gigantic are the leaves and blossoms, the more fantastic their forms. Water is plentiful; the very air is saturated with it, enabling some tropical plants to discard their roots entirely and climb up into the treetops!

Lowlands and mountains in the temperate zone reproduce somewhat the same contrasts as poles and equator. The plant, tree or shrub, which at the bottom of the mountain is tall and slender, grows shorter and stockier all the way up the mountainside, developing ever stronger roots, sparser foliage and smaller blossoms.

The strange forms of desert plants like the cacti teach the children further secrets of the world they live in. Cacti grow only where there is little interplay between earth and sky; the rhythmic mediation of rising moisture and falling rain is almost wholly lacking in the desert. Earth forces prevail, forming the plant into a distorted organism of roots and thick, leathery stalk. Nothing remains of the leaf part but the veins, which have become a dried-out skeleton, a group of spiny thorns. When blossoms develop, they look as though they had fallen from above and lodged by mere chance on top of the cactus, so unrelated are they to its other parts.

There are brief seasons when the heavens dip down and rains drench the desert. Then a great sea of blossoms springs up, and the wastelands are transformed almost overnight into green and flowering meadows.

Perhaps there is more than poetry in the resemblance we find between stars and blossoms!

Another strange member of the plant world offers a great contrast to the cactus. This is the mushroom, which like the cactus is essentially a stalk organism, but how different they are! Where the cactus is fairly firmly rooted the mushroom barely grazes the earth; where the cactus is hard, angular and contracted the mushroom is soft, round and swollen; where the cactus exists almost wholly without water but must have warmth and sunlight, the mushroom grows only in cool, dark, wet places.

In trees and shrubs with their hard wood and bark we find extensions of the mineral kingdom into the realm of living things. Leaves and blossoms grow from the hard stalk of trunk and branches as though from the soil itself. In wood the characteristic hardness of the mineral element has been wrought into living flexibility by its intrusion into the plant realm. When wood rots it falls away into a crumbling substance like sand, and we see it returning again to its native element.

Pictures of nature such as these nourish the child's imagination as well as inform him. They speak directly to his feeling. They lead him out into a new, warm connection with the world at a time when his developing ego-hood most threatens to cut him off and shut him up inside himself. Such a perspective on nature coming at this age is as curative and wholesome as it is instructive.

* * * * * *

Greek epics and legends form the chief reading and story-telling material and supplement the history of the fifth grade. A year ago the children would scarcely have appreciated these smooth classics. Now they have more feeling for finesse, and the adventurous spirit of the Greek heroes, which led them on such long hazardous voyages, is much akin to the ten-year-old's own need for wide perspectives.

At this time, when the child is developing a strong sense of his own personality, every opportunity is taken to teach him to respect that of others. He is helped to differentiate clearly and accurately between his own opinions and experiences and those of others in all his written and oral work. This emphasis is applied to grammar in the practice of direct and indirect quotation. The verb forms are studied and all personal mood, such as finds expression in punctuation, is taken up in conscious detail.

Fractions and decimals continue to be the chief concern of arithmetic study in the fifth grade. By now the children should feel quite at home with both and use them with considerable ease.

* * * * * *

Another new element introduced into the fifth grade curriculum in connection with the study of Greek civilization is the Greek language itself. Latin, too, is taken up in this grade and closely related to the learning of Greek. Both languages are treated from a purely musical-poetic angle throughout this first year. They are made an experience in main lesson subjects. Like the two modern languages, which are continued as before, they are given two short weekly periods apiece.

In music the children learn to read and write all the major and minor scales. Ear-training, polyphonic singing and flute-playing, music theory and appreciation continue.

Speech eurythmy lessons again emphasize the relation of grammar to movement. Rod and rhythmic exercises of an energetic kind are done to help the child with his coordination at this time of rapid growth.

Tone eurythmy closely parallels the music lessons. The major scales are practiced, and the rounds and canons sung in music periods are worked out in eurythmic form.

In handwork the children learn to knit gloves and stockings. Cloth dolls and animals are also made in connection with main lesson periods in geography and man and animal.

Physical education activities retain a strongly rhythmic character. Both eurythmy and physical education periods are doubled in this grade.

CHAPTER VII

The Eleven-Year-Olds

The development of the child from birth or conception to maturity has been described in the first chapter as an evolutionary process in which the human spirit gradually gains mastery over its bodily instrument. *This evolution is in the truest sense emergent.* Just as physical birth is literally an emergence terminating the period of fetal development and releasing the organism into an entirely new phase of maturation, so other less obvious births occur at intervals in what may be called a series of further emergences.

Significant laws govern this evolutionary process. Not only does each new birth free a new human capacity that heretofore existed only in embryonic form and was therefore not yet available for use. It introduces a new phase of development in which a still further germinal capacity is launched into an embryonic growth phase.

Recent psychological investigations have unearthed a wealth of evidence that document Steiner's great discovery that man's psychological as well as physical development proceeds in a series of metamorphoses. The concept of metamorphosis is absolutely fundamental to the Steinerian psychology and to the education based on it. According to this school of thought and observation, the whole human being is completely transformed with every step forward in his emergent evolution. Not only do bodily changes like those of birth, second dentition and puberty occur; psychic changes also take place, revolutionizing the individual's whole inner life. Capacities that have existed in one form become transmuted into capacities of another kind. Between the tenth and eleventh years, for example, the imaginative thinking characteristic of early childhood undergoes a metamorphosis from which it re-emerges as the ability to form abstract concepts. The change has been long in coming, for embryonic growth is a slow process of maturation. *But the time comes when the matrix of imagination within which the intellectual capacity has been ripening releases thought as a full-born power of the human spirit.* This is not to imply that the child has not thought before; he has thought, but his thinking has had a pictorial rather than a conceptual character.

Thought, then, is literally imagination's child. To understand this is to understand the emphasis placed on the cultivation of the child's imaginative powers in the Steiner elementary school curriculum.

It is indeed possible to force the thought capacity into premature birth and functioning. Schools of our time habitually do so, for adults can no longer conceive of any but conceptual thinking. Witness the fad for determining I.Q.'s that so recently swept the educational profession! Thought may indeed be forced, but to force it is to warp this finest of human powers for the rest of life, just as a pair of legs is permanently warped if a child is forced to walk before the time is ripe for such an attempt.

This *ripening in time* is a fundamental concept in understanding every aspect of human evolution. The curriculum of the Steiner schools is wholly based upon it. Studies are conceived as a support for normal growth and introduced into the curriculum at the time and in the way they may best serve that growth. Their character changes with the child's changing

86

capacities as he emerges into ever further phases of development.

The thinking that emerges as a ripened power from the matrix of a healthy imagination *is a warm and mobile thinking.* It is the fruit of the living pictures with which the world has been brought into the child's consciousness. These pictures have lived and grown with him. They have awakened his whole enthusiasm for the world about him. Abstract concepts would have done quite the opposite; they would have caused him to withdraw from the world prematurely in order to observe it accurately and then to generalize about it. If this withdrawal occurs too early, the individual becomes cold and critical; he has knowledge, but little wisdom. Furthermore, abstract concepts arrest the growth process, for they are essentially unchanging. They stiffen the child's soul, whereas pictures enhance its natural liveliness and keep it plastic. A child who is constantly being encouraged by his teachers to be a little scientist and to form abstract thoughts about everything he experiences is missing out on his childhood and becoming an old man before his time.

The ability to form abstract concepts is normally born in the late pre-adolescent period. For a time it lies rather weak and helpless like any newborn baby. Only at puberty does it really find its legs and begin to move freely about. In the meantime, it must receive fitting exercise. The curricula of the next three school years are shaped to provide it.

A significant though subtle physical maturation occurring approximately at eleven must be mentioned to complete the picture of this phase of development. From the age of eight or thereabouts the child is the very embodiment of unconscious grace. He moves with such lightness and agility that it scarcely seems as though he had a bone in his body. At about eleven this condition changes. The human spirit, which heretofore had established itself essentially in the mobile muscular organism,

87

now extends its mastery to the last, most resistant outpost of the material organism, the skeleton. At this age children begin to seem all framework. They grow angular and lanky, and one would think to observe their awkward movements that they were strangers to their own bodies. *In a sense they have really become so.* They are repeating the same struggle for physical mastery at another level that they first passed through at birth and then again at six when they were laying hold of their big muscles. It takes several years before they have their bony systems well in hand and feel at home again in their organisms. Indeed, some individuals obviously never quite regain their control after this crisis, and as education has not understood the nature of their problem it can do little to help them.

The first ten years of life then lead in a series of greater and lesser metamorphoses to the important moment at which the individual completes incarnation. In coming thus wholly to himself he becomes for the first time wholly separated from the world about him. At such a moment he can begin to think about the world in abstract concepts, for he is himself abstracted from it. His concepts now reflect the world as pictures did not. Pictures *revealed* the world to him in living symbols. They were neither reality itself nor mere reflections of reality as concepts are. Pictures were half-way between the child and reality. He *went out* into the pictures that the teacher offered him. Anyone who has ever told stories to a group of children has had opportunity to observe how they go out into the picture element and live in it quite outside themselves. In concepts, however, the world is no longer even half-real. It has become a reflection, a photograph. It has been reduced to a mere shadow of itself.

Now that he has entered this new state of consciousness and can live unharmed in the shadow realm of concepts because of the protection against this death element that his previous

88

education has given him, the child may be introduced to many new studies. He takes up black and white drawing for the first time and begins geometry, physics, geology and mineralogy. Many questions arise in him as to the how and why of things that had formerly been accepted without special notice. He has a real hunger to know the laws by which things work, especially if they have not been forced on his attention prematurely. But as he begins his intellectual development and studies the physical sciences for the first time, art also becomes a special study. Painting, modelling and charcoal drawing now occupy main lesson periods. Not that these activities are taken out of their connection with other learning; they continue to play their part in all other studies, but for the first time special artistic and technical problems of art are made the object of special study.

* * * * * *

Acoustics or sound theory is the first of the physical sciences to be taken up. Here the path leads from familiar experiences in tone and speech to experimentation with sound phenomena of other kinds. The children's attention is called to the element of beauty to be experienced in musical sound as they perform and listen to compositions they have grown to love. They try out tone combinations and distinguish between intervals that seem beautiful and others that are displeasing to the ear. How expressive each interval is when one listens carefully and plays it several times over! How mysteriously the prime is re-echoed in the octave! Yet there are subtle differences too. The children try to discover what these are. The second and seventh have a searching, questioning quality in common. The third and sixth are alike in expressing a certain contentment. The fourth is curiously prosaic, the fifth hollow as a bell. To play a succession of fifths gives one a strangely chilly feeling. It becomes

89

evident that musical sounds, like those of speech, always convey feeling experiences even when they are produced at random on an instrument. There is always a dramatic element in them, dreams and fulfillments, struggles, conflicts, friendliness, loneliness, rejoicing. Tones are like colors: all kinds of pictures come into being through their intermingling.

From tones created by the voices or instruments of human beings the children turn to the sounds of nature: to the voices of animals, birds and insects; to the soughing of the wind in reeds and branches, the rustling of leaves, the creaking of straining tree trunks; to the striking of rock on rock, the plunging of stones into quiet pools; to the ringing of hammered metals, the roaring of landslides, the tinkling or booming of ice in freezing lakes, the splashing of water, the strange dreaming tone of sea shells; the music of telephone wires. Careful distinctions are made between tones and noises.

After exploring the variety of sounds to be heard in nature, the children begin a series of experiments. They try out violin strings, discovering how certain divisions of the string produce certain definite intervals. If one divides the string exactly into halves, both halves resound as octaves of the tone produced by the string before it was divided. Other divisions result in other harmonies of relationships between the original tone and the tones made by subdivision. Expressed in fractions, these relationships are revealed in another way as number harmonies; concord and discord are perceived to be mathematical order and disorder. Such a discovery makes a child know that his ear has not deceived him into a purely subjective judgment of esthetic value, but that beauty is objective truth, and truth beauty.

Other instruments may also be used and the principles whereby tone changes are produced on them investigated. In addition to the violin, the children can easily experiment with woodwinds, using their own recorder-flutes, or they may make a simple drum to demonstrate the principle of tonal production in percussion instruments.

From a study of interrelationships, overtones and vibrations, the mathematical aspects of sound phenomena, the children proceed to problems of tone conduction. Some substances, like metals, allow sound to flow through them as easily as light flows through glass or other transparent media. Others, like wood, are opaque and resistant. All kinds of substances are experimented with and the tone-flow through them measured.

From these experiments with external sound phenomena the studies are led back to the human organism to a consideration of the structure and functioning of the ear and larynx.

* * * * * *

The world of light and color is so closely related to the world of tone that optical studies follow directly upon those in acoustics.

Optics, like acoustics, begins with familiar experiences in the realm of beauty. The colors that the children have been applying quite naively in their painting for the past several years are now observed more closely. Each color is studied for its own special attributes and then observed in relation to other colors. The children will notice how different each color combination is from every other. Some combinations are highly pleasing, others less so; some seem harmonious, some conflicting; some have a soothing quality, while others are positively irritating.

Turning to a study of color in the world about them the children naturally begin with the sun, the giver of light. They discover how light, which is itself invisible, strikes into darkness, and color is born of this meeting of two opposites. From the cosmic phenomena of light and darkness they go on to experiment with artificial light and shadow in the classroom;

91

they turn from the rainbow to the prism. They study how colors change with distance and with the medium through which one looks at them. They observe how differently light is related to the elements of earth, air and water; they distinguish between opaque and translucent substances. A number of experiments are performed to observe the phenomena and determine the laws of light refraction. The lens and the camera are studied. In all these studies the principles underlying the various light and color phenomena are arrived at as end products generalized from concrete experiences rather than stated theoretically before the experiments are made.

Children of this age are hardly able to enter into a study of the human eye. In the course of their experimenting, however, they discover a wonderful secret of its functioning; even this small part of the organism is so imbued with the human capacity for wholeness that to gaze at one color for a few moments is automatically to create an impression of the polar opposite that complements it.

*　*　*　*　*　*

History in the fifth grade was ancient history, the story of the cultural childhood of humanity told in pictures. It ended with a contemplation of Greek civilization at its flood-tide. Sixth grade history begins with the great turning point in human evolution when the bright glow of the golden age of Greece was fading and a new age dawned. It was in Greek times that men first began to question and to think for themselves; modern consciousness was born with the first scientific concepts formed by Greek thinkers. It was at the end of Greek civilization that Christ lived and died, and the history and culture of the whole modern world hinged on that event as they date from it.

The eleventh year is the ideal time to study the transition

from ancient to modern history, from a poetic consciousness warm in wisdom to a search for truth in the form of scientific concepts because the eleven-year-old is himself involved in a similar transition. He has left childhood behind when he enters into the adult thinking consciousness that is born at eleven. He is now able to grasp history as a temporal sequence of cause and effect relationships.

His historical studies now lead through the decline of Greece, the rise and fall of Rome to the effects of these two great cultures on European civilization up to the beginning of the fifteenth century, when once again a great stirring in men's souls drove them to seek new physical and spiritual horizons. Every effort should be made to make these studies so vivid that the children can enter fully into them with heart and feeling. The character of a period is best brought home by describing the destinies of real persons who helped to shape their time. There is tremendous drama in the contrast between the life-experience of a Phidias, Pericles or Alexander and that of Cicero or Tacitus, the Irish monk St. Gallus, the minnesinger Wolfram von Eschenbach, or Godfrey de Bouillon the crusader.

The cold plunge experienced in turning from the glorious warmth of Greek art and culture to a study of the rigid, legalistic minds of the Romans is more than made up for by the impressions the child receives of the gradual rising of the individual to entirely new stature, to new powers of mind, to the new ability to love his neighbor as himself that grew with the Christianizing of humanity.

* * * * * *

In geography the horizon is extended from the children's own country and its closest neighbors to more distant lands and people. Climate is studied, introducing the first astronomical concepts. The children now gain a clear picture of the

93

distribution of oceans, seas and continents and of the great mountain masses. It is pointed out how the mountain ranges of the western hemisphere lie in an essentially north-south orientation, while in Europe and Asia they extend along a west-east axis.

The plant and animal life in the regions under consideration is studied in relation to climatic conditions.

Map-making is given much attention and carried out with all possible artistry.

* * * * * *

Nature study, which hitherto was concerned wholly with the realm of life, now turns from the plant world to the mineral kingdom. The children are reminded that they are actually standing on this fourth kingdom of nature so different from the living kingdoms they have come to know in man, plants and animals. They feel how solid the earth is beneath their feet and how good it is to have this firm foundation providing support for the development of the three higher kingdoms.

The difference between soft limestone, which had its origin in living organisms, and granite, the hardest of minerals, is then discussed. The children learn the location of the great limestone and granite masses of the earth, linking this study to their previous geographical conceptions. From this larger perspective they proceed to a consideration of the type of rock underlying their own portion of the globe.

The structure of the earth is then pictured, beginning with its mantles of warmth, light and air extending many miles above our heads. Next comes the earth's surface with human beings and animals moving over it; then the vegetation growing out of layers of humus, loam, clay, sand and even stone. Finally, there is the great rock body of the earth with veins of ore running through it and at its core the primeval fire burning and forcing its way up to the surface in volcanoes. The forming of granite mountains through the fiery forces of eruption is contrasted with the creation of limestone ranges through erosion. The parts played by the fiery and watery elements in the forming of the earth's present features are followed through the geological ages. The various layers of rock are discussed and identified.

From a study of rocks and the flora and fauna of the geological ages the children go on to minerals, metals and finally gems and crystals, the most perfect products of the mineral kingdom. The attributes and qualities of the various metals are compared and their use in human life explored. Metals and gems, which are surrounded by an aura of such mystery and romance, have played a remarkable role throughout history. As they are studied some of the poetry and legend that has arisen around them is brought into the lessons. The forms and certain aspects of the chemical composition of crystals are examined and discussed. The six-sided quartz crystal, for example, is compared with the hexagonal snowflake and the honey cell. Last comes the diamond, that wonder of the mineral world that has been transformed from a black, opaque vegetable substance into the hardest, most brilliant and transparent of white crystals. Such a stone is bound to awaken deep awe in those who contemplate it and to stand as an eternal symbol of all things rare and precious.

Explorations of the mineral kingdom lead back at last to man, to the presence of mineral and metallic substances in the human organism and the use made of them in the body's economy.

* * * * * *

Mathematics plays an exceptional role in the child's development. It is at once the most abstract and the most practical of skills and subjects; it is pure truth and beauty, yet it has its application in the most prosaic fields of human activity. In teaching mathematics care should be taken to give the children the widest possible experience of both these aspects, to let them feel how number plays into every phase of human living.

Properly taught, mathematics endears itself greatly to the children. It comes to seem a realm of almost magical possibilities. It is important that enthusaism should be felt for this subject, for mathematics is the means whereby thought attains keenness and mobility. It is a trainer of the sense of truth.

The mathematics of the sixth grade branches out in practical, abstract and esthetic directions. Banking problems are taken up, and the wide variety of arithmetical applications with which the children have been concerned is reduced to algebraic formulae. Geometrical design, which formerly had more the character of free, artistic drawing, now becomes practice with instruments and is done with utmost accuracy. "Families" of geometric figures are constructed and studied for the numerical laws which they embody. A wealth of flower and leaf forms emerges from this work in geometric construction, making the children realize afresh how all creation is permeated by the number element.

Modelling too takes up the theme of geometric forms, and the children model spheres, cubes, pyramids and other more complicated polyhedric figures.

No theorems are taught as such in the sixth grade, though they are demonstrated visually. Everything that will later become a purely mental exercise in abstract mathematical reasoning is thus first concretely experienced.

Perspective drawing is introduced in the sixth grade in connection with geometric drawing, out of which it is developed.

* * * * * *

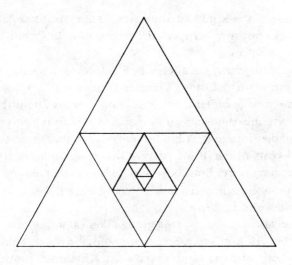

A Family of Triangles

English lessons continue to emphasize grammar with a view to acquainting the children with the full color and plasticity of speech. Business English is developed as a continuation of letter-writing practice.

The reading matter of the sixth grade goes hand in hand with the study of history, which it supplements and enriches.

All four languages are continued. The children begin reading the two modern languages for the first time. Greek and Latin are also read, but the spoken word still receives the chief emphasis. Short texts, fables, poems and legends are learned by heart. Short descriptive sentences are translated into all four languages if the teacher as well as the children are equal to it, and interesting differences and similarities in words and structure are noted. Such exercises bring to light the cultural backgrounds out of which the languages developed.

In music the study of the minor scales begins. All other activities continue, supported by corresponding tone-eurythmic experiences.

Speech eurythmy parallels English lessons in a study of style and grammatical forms. There is further exploration of the movement of geometric patterns. Rod exercises help the children overcome the awkwardness that is a natural result of their stage of development. It has been my experience, however, that several years of eurythmy prevent this crisis in grace from becoming too severe. Both boys and girls usually pass through it without a conspicuous loss of coordination because it has become second nature.

Physical education in this grade takes on a more gymnastic character. All kinds of exercises for conscious body control are done, with and without apparatus. Rhythmic jumping in group sequences is practiced. Javelin throwing, hurdling, broad and high jumping are introduced.

Woodworking is added to the handwork activities. The children learn to carve simple articles of household use and to design and make toys and moving parts.

Another important study, farming or gardening, is introduced into this year's curriculum. If possible the children go out to a real farm for this period and learn every kind of farm work. They develop a group fruit and vegetable garden, which they plough, plant, cultivate and harvest themselves. The patient effort involved in raising farm produce is a wholesome social experience for the children.

CHAPTER VIII

The Twelve-Year-Olds

It will be noted that every subject in the Waldorf curriculum begins and ends with man. Learning is kept the warm concern it should be and made a diet by which the whole child is nourished.

Warmth theory, which is taken as a seventh grade main lesson subject, accordingly begins with the phenomena of warmth in human experience. The child will have noticed his own bodily warmth and how mysteriously it maintains itself against outer coldness. Perhaps he has handled other creatures; warm-blooded ones like his cat or dog, or cold frogs, snakes and fishes, and felt what a difference there can be in respect to their body temperatures. Sometimes he has had fever and felt the heat surging uncomfortably through his body.

Then, too, he has experienced another kind of warmth, the warmth of affection, the fire of enthusiasm. Such feelings make his heart glow inside him like a sun. He has seen this inner sun light up other people's faces and literally shine out of them. In olden times men spoke of the heart as the sun within, for it is both a warmth and a light-giver in the inner man.

The outer world, too, is full of warmth processes. There the sun is the great warmth source. All living creatures love the sun's heat. They hide away in the cold months when the sun is too far away to warm them, and then come out to bask in it when spring brings it near again.

99

Not only living things are affected by the sun's warmth. The rocks, the water, the air change too, expanding with an increase in heat and contracting under the influence of coldness. Water shows this most clearly. When water is heated, it becomes a gas that we see disappearing into the air in clouds of mist. When it is cooled sufficiently, it becomes a solid.

All sorts of experiments can be made with gases, liquids and solids to demonstrate the effect of heat and cold on these three elements. Some interesting generalizations can then be made. It is found that solids are the rugged individualists among substances, for each solid has an individual shape and an individual rate of expansion. Liquids, too, have individual expansion, but they all have the same shape in common: they are all horizontal. Gases have both shape and expansion rate in common.

Solid, liquid and gaseous substances are experimented with to determine their burning qualities and the color and composition of the flame. Heat conduction tests and measurements are made. Warmth is discovered to be the most mobile as it is the most elusive of the elements. Wherever it is applied to a substance it brings it into motion, causing it to expand and eventually to boil and circulate. Blood, the carrier of warmth in man and the higher mammals, is the most mobile part of the organism, coursing ceaselessly through the body. When one grows warmer the blood flows faster. People who grow hot with anger typically speak of their blood "boiling with rage."

From these discoveries of the nature of warmth in their own bodies and the outer world the children go on to explore some of the common uses to which this lively element is put in man's service.

* * * * * *

Acoustical and optical studies are carried further in the seventh grade. Other physical sciences taken up in the physics main lesson periods are electricity, magnetism and mechanics. The interesting history of the discovery and use of magnetism and electricity is told. The children make experiments and learn the fundamental laws and the modern uses of these two still highly mysterious forces.

Mechanics begins with the lever principle as this is found in the human arm. From their experimentation the children learn the basic mechanical concepts and their application in the machinery of ancient and modern times.

* * * * * *

Chemistry is also introduced into the seventh grade in an elementary way as a study of combustive processes. The beautiful legend of the bringing of fire to the earth by Prometheus, who lit a torch at the sun's blazing chariot, is told, and a vivid word-picture is painted of this fierce consuming element with its licking tongues of flame.

It is not a long step from such a picture to a study of combustion in the human organism. Combusion is found to be a process whereby substances are digested and changed into other forms. This same digestive process, which in the human body changes the form of the foods one has eaten and releases warmth and energy, can be observed externally in the breaking down of substances by fire. Fire is literally a digester. As the children's experiments will show, fire changes the form of the substances that they subject to burning. It digests them, freeing heat and gases into the atmosphere and leaving nothing but mineral sediment behind in the form of ashes. Fire, the child of the sun, thus restores to the sun the organic substances that its life-giving rays once brought into being. Fire restores to the earth the mineral ash that was of the earth's own body.

Experiments in which organic and inorganic substances are first weighed and then subjected to burning show by the ash residue what part life had in their building and what part the

101

lifeless element. How thrilling it is, after having learned some of the secrets of the plant world, to subject root, stalk, leaf and blossom to trial by fire and to see in the minute proportion of ash yielded by burned blossoms that they are indeed cosmic visitors to earth, while the earth-dwelling root has by far the greatest proportion of minerals!

These first chemical concepts supplement the children's social, scientific and nature studies in a way that makes it possible to unite them all in a comprehensive survey of production, distribution and consumption in the modern world.

* * * * * *

Astronomy has already been introduced in connection with the study of climate in sixth grade geography. In the seventh grade it is taken as a main lesson subject and extended to give the children a picture of world space. From their own place on the earth the children can observe the sun's movement from sunrise to sunset, the wheeling of the stars across the sky by night. They contrast these movements as seen in the temperate zone with the movements of the same bodies perceived at the poles and equator and draw the wholly different lines thus obtained. Their observation of solar, lunar, planetary and stellar phenomena leads them to a picturing of world-spatial relationships.

A wealth of stories, legends and poems about the stars is interwoven with these studies.

* * * * * *

Nature study in the seventh grade returns to man. The physiology of the life processes, blood circulation, respiration and nutrition is taken up and studied in connection with health and hygiene. Eleven-year-old children are well able to grasp these processes. Moreover, at this age it is possible for them to enter into health studies with a freshly impersonal scientific interest that prevents their falling victim to the faddism and self-interest so characteristic of older persons' concern with this subject.

* * * * * *

Seventh grade history is an intensive study of the Renaissance, that great turning-point in the evolution of human consciousness. The ferment that worked in men's souls at that time, bringing all previous cultural achievements to a final glorious flowering, also ushered in a new age of wide scientific inquiry and exploration. No period of history is more alive with drama. The people of the times were intensely colorful, dramatic figures; there is a fabulous quality in their personalities and life-experience. Here history is truly at its most story-like.

Geography, which now runs parallel with history, takes up the theme of adventurous exploration and covers the whole globe. The children's knowledge of astronomy is called upon to further their understanding of climate and its effect upon the cultural and economic life of the various peoples of the earth.

* * * * * *

In English the study of the plastic shaping of speech in expressions of wish, surprise, command, etc., is continued. Reading material is again taken largely from the field of historical literature, while composition leads into problems of style in descriptions of nature. The children's practical sense is further cultivated in a continued study of business English.

* * * * * *

Lines of Consecutive Star Positions
(as drawn by H. von Baravalle)

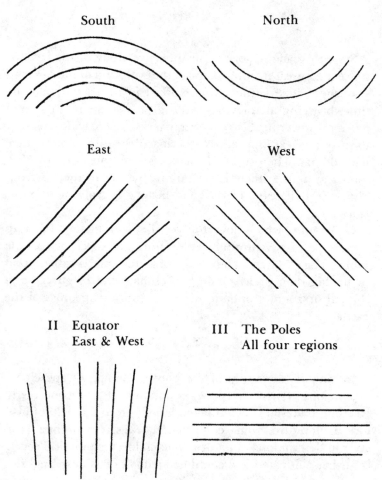

I   New York, Lat. 41°

South   North

East   West

II   Equator
     East & West

III   The Poles
      All four regions

Mathematics introduces work with negative numbers for the first time. It is a significant experience for the child to venture into this realm of mathematical thinking that has no relation to physical perceptions and therefore makes real demands on his imaginative powers.

Square and cube root and ratio are also introduced. The study of algebra and business arithmetic continues.

Geometrical and perspective drawing is continued in more complex form. Instruction in geometry is still entirely visual, as in the sixth grade.

* * * * * *

Foreign language lessons now consist largely of a survey of the literature of both languages, carried out in connection with a study of the style of life and speech of the two peoples. Latin and Greek continue to be taught in the same informal spirit as before. Grammar studies in these languages are incidental rather than systematic.

Music introduces a capella singing, and a special study is made of older polyphonic folk tunes. Theoretical studies are continued. The children learn the simpler forms of composition. Their acquaintance with the works of the great masters is extended and made the basis of a study of musical style.

Both tone and speech eurythmy continue to support musical, language and geometrical studies. The children accompany each other when instrumental compositions are worked out in tone eurythmy practice.

Handwork lessons are devoted chiefly to sewing. Both boys and girls design and make some article of clothing. The girls do the embroidering of their own and the boys' creations. A study of the different weaves and materials is made.

Physical education takes on a decidedly gymnastic character, putting its emphasis on control and precision. Rhythmic group

105

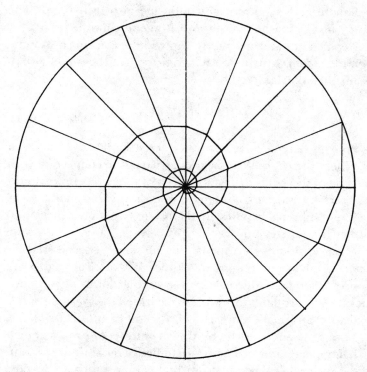

A spiral made by consecutive perpendiculars.

exercises in running, jumping and javelin throwing continue and extensive use is made of all types of indoor and outdoor apparatus. Sports and national games are played with the single exception of football and soccer, which make an unnatural use of the limbs and head.

*   *   *   *   *   *

No mention has been made above of religious education. Wherever possible this is carried out by pastors of the various denominations for the children of their religious communities. Periods and classrooms are provided by the school for this purpose. For those children whose parents wish it, general instruction of a Christian kind is given by the class teachers in all eight grades. In the first grade fairy tales with their potent moral pictures are the sole content of the religious lessons. Second grade introduces legends of saints and other persons of great moral beauty. The next three grades study the poetry and stories of the Old and New Testaments. The sixth grade reads biographies of outstanding human beings who struggled and endured greatly in the service of humanity. The seventh and eighth grades read the four Gospels.

A simple and beautiful service is conducted for the school on Sunday by members of the faculty wherever possible. It makes a deep impression on the children to have the same teachers officiating at these ceremonies who on weekdays have taught them business English or embroidery or gardening. Such an experience offers them pictures of whole human beings rather than of specialists.

Reverence is not a virtue left for Sunday cultivation in a Steiner school, however. It goes hand in hand with knowledge and is the constantly resounding overtone of every study.

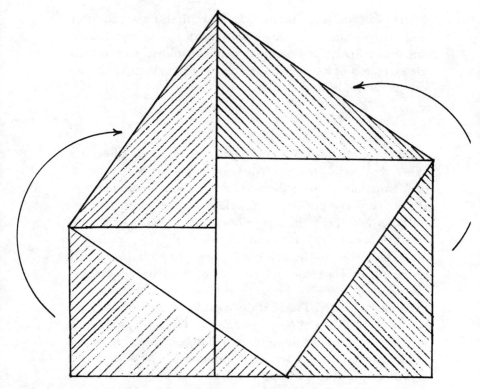

"The square on the hypotenuse of a right triangle is equal to the sum of the squares on the two other sides" visually demonstrated.

CHAPTER IX

The Thirteen-Year-Olds

In the light of the Steinerian principle of metamorphosis the development of the human being from birth to twenty-one falls into three great growth-phases, each one of which requires a different type of education. In the first phase, lasting until the onset of second dentition, the world is the child's teacher. He lives wholly imbedded in his surroundings, learning by imitation and drinking in impressions with keen, wide-open senses. At this age it would be presumptuous to instruct him. It is enough to provide him with impressions of a human world of goodness, truth and beauty. For the rest, nature herself cares for him as no human being can. If circumstances make it necessary for him to attend a nursery school or kindergarten he will be endlessly content to play there with a few simple playthings. He builds in the sandbox or works over a doll's house by the hour. Perhaps he will sing with other children, listen to a story, or join in a vigorous eurythmy game for a short while. He will be delighted to see pots of paint on the table and to be allowed to dip his brush into them and spread the lovely colors on his paper. But let no one attempt to organize his learning or to interpret the world to him. Though he asks endless questions, learned answers enter his ears as so much empty air or at best as a kind of soothing music. He does not want to be taught . He is too busy learning to welcome interruptions, and his keen senses perceive far more than we know how to teach him.

With the maturation that takes place at five or six, however, the child begins to withdraw from the world into the fastnesses of his own being. Slowly the world becomes a riddle to him. Now he has a real need of knowledge. At this period we do well to offer him instruction, to bring the world to him provided we can do so as artists in pictures that speak potently of reality.

In the third great phase that follows upon puberty the child's thinking powers have become fully emancipated. From now on he needs to be taught in clear-cut concepts. Only specialists in every field of subject matter are now equal to the task of answering his keen questions and commanding his respect. From this time forward his schooling changes radically. He no longer has the same teacher for all his lessons. Though his curriculum continues to be organized in blocks of main lesson periods in an extensive variety of academic and technical subjects—supplemented by languages, art, handwork, carpentry and gardening—he is now a mature student visiting the classrooms of experts in each field.

Human growth in the three major phases of childhood may be likened to three movements of a symphony or to plant growth with its three motives of root, leaf-stalk and blossom development. Each phase has its entirely distinctive character. Yet there is a living continuity that builds the three parts into one whole and perfect organism.

It is important that each growth-phase receive proper cultivation. This means developing the human power that emerges with each new maturation. If this is not done when the time is ripe, the opportunity is lost forever, and the child is irrevocably denied the possibility of full human growth.

*   *   *   *   *   *

The second phase of childhood corresponds approximately to the eight year period of elementary schooling. This is the phase with which this volume has been concerned. The further education provided for in the Waldorf curriculum can only be adequately described by the specialists who now become the children's teachers at the high school level.

It is the task of elementary education to give children in the second phase of maturation an understanding of man and the world they live in, to offer them knowledge so rich and warm as to engage their hearts and wills as well as minds. Such an understanding is the basis of all real efficiency in later years. Children educated in Rudolf Steiner's sense are genuinely practical as well as finely artistic human beings.

With the completion of the eighth grade the children should have a well-rounded general picture of man and universe. This last year should not only bring all previous experiences to a new peak, but enable the children to enter fully and potently into the life of their own times.

In accordance with these aims, history becomes a broad survey of the cultural development of humanity, culminating in an intensive study of the industrial revolution that has so radically changed human life in the last three centuries. Geography takes up the same theme, showing the role played by every part of the earth in modern industrial civilization. A comprehensive picture is given of the relation of mineral resources and plant and animal life to the life of human beings in the various regions of the earth.

Physics lessons complement these historical and geographical surveys. The practical uses made of man's new knowledge of all the physical sciences are thoroughly explored. In addition to further studies in optics and acoustics, thermodynamics, mechanics, electricity and magnetism, the children are now introduced to hydraulics, aerodynamics and meteorology.

111

The sciences are approached experimentally rather than theoretically in every case, and the lessons culminate in considerations of the practical value and significance for human life of the forces involved.

Chemistry is also considered in relation to industry. In addition, the children learn something of organic chemistry. Fats, sugars, proteins and starches are identified and a study is made of the roles they play in the building of organic substances.

Mathematics also emphasizes the practical applications of arithmetic, algebra and geometry. Demonstrations in plane and solid geometry lead to problems in the measurement of surfaces and volume. The study of graphs is introduced.

*   *   *   *   *   *

Man is again the subject of nature study. The structure and functions of the three systems that make up the human organism are observed in great detail from the standpoint of form and movement. It is shown, for example, how the function of the head is one of intake. Four of the five physical senses are built into the head as perceptive organs. The solid bone of the skull is penetrated by a number of small openings through which impressions of the outer world may enter. Even the mouth, the representative of the limb-metabolic system in the head described in chapter five, is an organ of intake, whereas the metabolic system has the entirely opposite function of transforming and distributing. This is the pole of outgoing processes, of radiation. The chest or thorax, the center of the body's rhythmic functions, holds the balance between intake and outgo, just as it holds a balance between the head's roundness and the limbs' linear structure.

The head is the still, cold pole of the organism, in contrast to the mobile, warmth-producing, combustive process of digestion. It is interesting to note how this esoteric fact is recognized in colloquial expressions. We describe someone contemptuously as "hot-headed" or we praise someone else by saying that he "has a cool head on his shoulders." We recognize the principle of stillness embodied in the head when we say, "I stopped to think."

It is a wonderful experience for the children to realize how man holds the contrasting functions of his threefold organism in perfect balance, to learn that health depends on his ability to do so. If the withholding tendency normal to the head lays hold on the digestive system, illness is the immediate result. If metabolic processes overstep their bounds, warmth floods the organism and the whole body is consumed by fever in a caricature of the digestive process. The rhythmic processes are then caught up in exaggerated motion; the head is invaded by an unnatural pressure from within and one feels as though one's skull were splitting. The role of the rhythmic organism as an essential mediator becomes clear in the light of these stark contrasts.

The children then proceed from this larger picture of the organism to more detailed studies. The muscular system, the nerves and lastly the skeleton are considered from the standpoint of both form and function. The differences between the human arm and leg structures are especially interesting to the children after their preliminary study of man and animal.

The eye, that most mechanically functioning of human sense organs, is the last part of the organism to be studied.

The children's attention is then drawn to the relation of man to the three lower kingdoms. It is pointed out that both the human and the vegetable kingdoms have the vertical principle in common, while the animal and mineral kingdoms are horizontally oriented. The plant, however, has its mouth in the ground and its reproductive organs at the top; its nutritional stream flows upward. In this sense it has an orientation exactly opposite to that of man.

The mineral kingdom has least relation to the human being;

form is the only element they share in common. The plant adds those of growth and reproduction; the animal, consciousness, but man alone is a self-conscious being. In this self-consciousness lie the grounds of his potential freedom and his responsibility.

* * * * * *

English lessons take up the theme of human freedom implicit in a study of epic and dramatic literature. Only at puberty, when the child has become a fully self-conscious individual, does he have any real feeling for the development of a personality through the repercussions of his own actions.

Business English receives a special emphasis in this grade.

The element of drama is also introduced into the children's work in speech eurythmy. Ballads are studied, and every eurythmic means of dramatic characterization offered by serious and humorous poetry is explored.

Music continues as in the seventh grade. In tone eurythmy the children complete the study of the minor scales. Polyphonic compositions with strong major and minor contrasts are worked out.

Painting concerns itself for the first time with highly conscious studies of highlights and shadows. Landscapes are painted with a view to atmospheric coloring. Modelling goes hand in hand with nature study; portrait heads or hands are now attempted. Drawing continues with an increased emphasis on beauty and functionality in technical designing.

The children's acquaintance with the literature and development of the two modern languages is extended, and they begin a study of poetry and metric forms. In Latin and Greek, longer works of great prose and poetry writers are read. There is still no systematic grammar study in the classical languages.

In handwork the children are taught machine sewing, iron-

114

ing and the use of the mangle. They learn to darn and patch. Artistic hand-sewing projects continue as before. Carpentry lessons are devoted to big projects extending over a number of weeks and requiring real skill and imagination on the children's part.

Physical education introduces wrestling and falling techniques. Rhythm is emphasized in all group exercises such as running, jumping and javelin throwing. Work with apparatus and sports continues as in the seventh grade.

* * * * * *

Perhaps this meagre sketch of the Waldorf elementary school curriculum may serve at least to clarify the educational philosophy and psychology that underlie it. Such a clarification may enable those who are striving for a solution of present day educational problems to make a fruitful use of Steiner's insight into human nature and development.

Dr. Richard Price, an American educational philosopher of Revolutionary times, wrote the following touching sentence in his book, *Observations on The Importance of The American Revolution*. "I have thought there may be a *secret* remaining to be discovered in education which will cause future generations to grow up virtuous and happy and accelerate human improvements to a greater degree than can at present be imagined." Those who know Steiner's work are convinced that he has discovered a fundamental secret of education that may yet richly justify the faith held by Dr. Price and others in the power of education to re-make the world.

CHAPTER X

The Temperaments

Psychology has been wrestling since the time of Aristotle with the problem of classifying human beings into groups or types. Extraordinary difficulties have always attended these labors of the typologist because no matter how many categories have been set up to accomodate human diversity no one quite fitted into any pattern. Individuals of supposedly confirmed "intellectual" traits might suddenly exhibit traces of "emotional" or "volitional" dispositions. Personalities thought to be of the "religious" type proved on occasion to possess marked "theoretical" or "economic" attributes. "Extroverts" had a way of turning into "introverts" and introverts into extroverts without the slightest warning, changing their temperamental coloring like the chameleon in response to appropriate stimuli in their environment. Psychologists have now generally recognized that it is impossible to confine any personality to a single category, and are therefore turning their attention to the unique rather than the similar qualities of human beings.

Within certain limits, however, there is admittedly much to be said for typology. Findings in this field have decided practical value for parents and educators among others, since they are constantly confronted with problems arising from their children's dispositions. In the case of children, unique personality has not yet had time to ripen fully, and type or temp-

116

erament is therefore especially pronounced. Often it is extreme enough to require special educational therapy.

Rudolf Steiner made the temperaments an object of intensive study. Although his typology went far beyond that of the Greeks and had none of its peculiar limitations, he found some aspects of the Greek conception adequate and so retained them. Like the Greeks he distinguished four temperaments which he designated choleric, sanguine, melancholic, and phlegmatic in accordance with traditional usage. Of these the melancholic disposition is most clearly introverted, the sanguine extroverted, while the phlegmatic and choleric temperaments partake in some respects of both introvert and extrovert tendencies.

Steiner's research resulted in findings of inestimable value for the practical handling of children's dispositions. Some of these findings must be included in even the briefest sketch of his educational methods.

As Steiner pointed out, the temperaments find characteristic expression in bodily as well as psychic attributes. The choleric child, for example, tends to be short and stocky, with a bull-neck and rounded head held rigid on his shoulders. He is extremely sturdy and possessed of untiring energy. He dominates his companions, assuming the role of ring-leader in all group activities. It is not easy to make an impression on him. If provoked, he explodes like a volcano. His wrathful outbursts easily degenerate into fits of frenzy. The choleric child is one-sided, egotistical, fanatic. It will be hard to disturb his self-confidence.

The melancholic child is in many respects the direct opposite of the choleric. He is tall for his age, lanky-limbed and slender, with a small, elongated head and sloping shoulders. He tends to suffer from anemia. Every experience makes a deep impression and sets him to brooding. Though his thoughtful nature leads him to develop a rich and interesting inner life, he is usually too shy to disclose it. He plays by himself, reads a

117

great deal, and is often gifted in music, poetry and painting.

Both the retiring disposition of the melancholic and the egotistical self-centeredness of the choleric tend to make children of these temperaments antisocial.

The phlegmatic child is fat and dumpy. He looks like a plump little bear always on the point of curling up for a winter's sleep. His laziness is the despair of his elders. Only a clap of thunder can stir his inertia. Yet he is a pleasant, thoroughly good-natured person. If the company is not so stimulating as to arouse him from his comfortable drowsing he will take part in social intercourse. A quiet sewing-circle is his metier.

The sanguine child is the most normally proportioned. He has small, nimble hands and feet that are seldom still. Every passing impression distracts his attention. He is unable to concentrate, tiring perceptibly when called upon to do so. His color comes and goes with his interest. Sanguine children are lovers of gaiety. They are the bright spots in the classroom.

In choleric children whose forceful, angry natures make them appear like snorting bulls, it is obvious that will is predominant. They love to put lots of red into their paintings. In music they prefer to play solo instruments.

In melancholic children thought is especially active. They are born scholars and philosophers. Soft blues and violets tend to predominate in their paintings. In the personal expression of solo singing these children find fitting musical release for the deep inwardness of their natures.

Sanguine children abandon themselves to feeling; they are easily moved to tears or laughter. There is a bird-like character in their flitting interest and nervous energy. They delight in color contrasts, though yellow is their special favorite. Their need of variety will be satisfied by nothing less than a whole orchestra of musical instruments.

Phlegmatic children are the most balanced of all four types. If only they could be roused from their lethargy! They sit in the classroom like gold-fish in a bowl, all lazy indifference. In painting they like a nice restful green; in music, choral singing, with its minimum of individual exertion.

Fortunately no child is restricted to a single temperament. The predominating disposition will usually be softened by a stronger or weaker admixture of the other three.

Often, as a child grows older, his temperament changes radically. The predominant characteristic may retire into the background and another previously less pronounced one take its place. Yet as a rule one basic temperament prevails throughout a lifetime.

Individual temperament may be modified by the dispositions characteristic of the different stages of maturity. Childhood is life's springtime or sanguine period; youth its warm-blooded, choleric summer; responsible, thoughtful maturity its melancholic autumn; old age its phlegmatic winter. Normal human beings take on the temperamental coloring natural to their years, and this enhances or subdues their individual tendencies.

The teacher will find allies as well as obstacles in his pupils' temperaments. He will rejoice, not in "small classes" and "homogeneous grouping," but in a large number and variety of children. His strength lies in the completeness of the human spectrum, of the orchestra of temperaments with which he is to work.

After a preliminary study of the children's traits he will proceed to seat them in advantageous portions of the classroom. The phlegmatic group will be placed at the front in order that the teacher's activity may go on right under their noses. The choleric ones will occupy rear seats where their disturbing influence makes itself least felt. This will not hinder their energy from leaping over the groups in front when class instruction is given. The melancholic children will be seated in the center by the windows where events outside will help to draw them out of their brooding. They will be less harmfully affected by distractions than children of the three other temperaments. The sanguine children may be placed next the inside wall. The more balanced ones of all four groups will provide good borders to soften the impact where one group touches upon another.

It may seem that these seating arrangements will only strengthen the children in their temperamental weaknesses. In practice the very opposite is true. This homogeneous grouping within the larger group brings each child face to face with his own one-sided characteristics. He stares at himself as though in a mirror, and soon becomes bored with his disposition. Slowly he will begin to develop other sides of his nature. The choleric, for example, must always be punching someone. Far better that he punch a choleric neighbor and they fight it out than that he pummel a melancholic child who will become all the more retiring under such treatment, tempting his tormentor to further assaults.

In this way the children themselves are brought to work upon their weaknesses. This is the only remedy. Fault-finding on the part of the teacher only defeats his purpose of bringing their natures into greater balance.

It will be necessary for the teacher to observe his pupils closely and to re-seat them if he finds evidence of changed conditions.

These seating measures provide the teacher with economical means of handling the wide diversity normally found in large classes. They enable him to individualize as well as to generalize his teaching.

While giving group instruction, the teacher utilizes this diversity to enrich the lesson for all four groups. In presenting his material he will deliberately turn to the sanguine children, who are all eager interest, and ask them to notice what he has drawn or written on the blackboard. Then he may call upon the choleric ones to come forward and demonstrate something to the others, or to work out the solution to some problem he has raised. The melancholic children will be pondering all the while, and with tactful encouragement may be brought to offer comments on the material that has been presented. The phlegmatic group will be the hardest to handle. Often the teacher may have to resort to artificial thunder-claps to waken them. He may drop a book, or jostle a chair or table to startle them, seizing the next five minutes to work with them intensively. The situation is rarely so extreme, however, as to require these harsher measures.

Since the phlegmatic children present the greatest problem the teacher will be especially concerned with them. Yet he dare not show this interest externally because it would only cause them to cease pulling on the oars altogether and to make him do all the work. He will stimulate them rather by his occasional dull indifference when dealing with them. When someone of their number makes a bad mistake, he may show that he has noticed it, but he turns away as though it did not interest him. This is not cold indifference, however; it is studied apathy. The surprise and uncertainty felt by the children at such moments will, if administered in homeopathic doses, prove effective in rousing these lazy little sleepers from their torpor.

Just the opposite with choleric children. Here the teacher's interest must be outwardly evident, while inwardly he strives to maintain a perfect calmness even if a child falls into a fury and begins to break up the furniture. He will quietly prevent damage if possible, but not allow himself to become enraged. To do so would only heap more coals on the child's burning mood and incite him to still greater offenses. He may instead make some grave comment summing up the situation, such as, "I see that you have thrown ink at Susie. Now her dress is ruined." A day or so later when the child himself has forgotten the outrage, the teacher will speak with him alone and recall the scene in its minutest detail. In the child's sobered state an objective picturing of his offensive behavior will call forth a wholesome sense of shame. Provision will also be made for the child himself to make good any damage he has done, if necessary earning the money to pay for it. It is important that no loving parent relieve him of this responsibility.

Other means are at the teacher's disposal for meeting the children's weaknesses and transforming them into strengths. The melancholic child, for example, is always absorbed in his own sorrows. He feels that no one but he was ever called upon to endure such suffering. If the teacher tries to cheer him up by being jolly, the child only feels the more isolated with his misery. Critical moments in his career present opportunities for story-telling of a kind especially suited to drawing him out of his self-absorption. The teacher may invent a story in which some character is forced to undergo the harshest trials, meeting them with noble fortitude. Or he may find such material in the biographies of historic personages. Such recitals awaken a kindred feeling in the melancholic child. They give him a sense of belonging to a large group of human beings who have suffered greatly and yet found it possible to turn their hard fortune into gain. The compassion he feels for them cures him of his own depression.

The same story may be retold with slightly different emphasis for the benefit of choleric children. They love to hear tales of great heroes and leaders who accomplished the impossible and led great numbers of people to a better life.

Such repetition is especially valuable, for it impresses the children with the many-sidedness of human nature.

Every subject may likewise be presented and repeated with the emphasis that most challenges the interest of the four temperaments. In geography, for example, the sanguine children have an especially keen interest in the variety of the earth's structure, climate, vegetation, and animal and human populations. The choleric ones are arrested by the drama of the elements, the force of wind and water, volcanoes, earthquakes and geysers, the upthrust or sinking of mountain ranges. They love to model regions of the earth's surface in relief, whereas the sanguine children prefer to paint detail maps in all possible color contrasts. The phlegmatic children love the flat, restful plains, the quiet lakes, the broad oceans, the gently flowing rivers and canals. Melancholic children are particularly impressed with man's responsibility for conserving natural resources and using them to improve our human lot to best advantage.

The secret of effective handling of the temperaments lies, not in suppressing, but rather in working positively with them. The sanguine child, for example, has a real need of variety. Similarly with the others, if their need is consistently satisfied, they will be ready of their own accord to reach out beyond their native limitations.

Moreover, the teacher's recognition and use of the strength of each temperament during class instruction periods enables the group as a whole to achieve a well-rounded balance that will have potent effect on individual development.

* * * * * *

Parents and teachers also have temperaments, and they will do well to recognize them and take steps toward attaining greater balance because children, especially in their younger years, are highly sensitive to the impressions that adult behavior makes upon them. Temperament colors speech, thought and gesture. It will reveal itself in the way a teacher reacts to schoolroom situations, in his mannerisms, in the way he grasps the chalk, in the listlessness or energy with which he uses it. All these impressions go deep into the child's physical organism.

The choleric teacher or parent who is given to sudden, violent bursts of fury causes his children to live in a perpetual state of subconscious terror. This fear will have crippling effect, not only on their childish good spirits, but on their digestive processes. We all know how anxiety upsets the stomach. Such a condition prolonged over a period of time disorganizes the bodily functions. As Dr. Steiner pointed out, it will show itself in later years as a tendency to gout or rheumatism.

The phlegmatic teacher has an equally drastic though more subtle effect on his pupils. Their lively spontaneity is repressed in his presence. This makes them fidgety and restless. At times they may even have outbursts of wild behavior. Nervous disorders may be the direct result of habitual resistance to a phlegmatic nature.

The melancholic teacher who is absorbed in his brooding fails to set up a reciprocal relationship with his pupils. He deprives them of that warmth and interest that is the very breath of classroom companionship between teacher and pupils. Children feel suffocated in such an atmosphere. Irregularities in the rhythmic interplay of breathing and blood circulation may be traced to this childhood deprivation.

The excessively sanguine teacher continually overstimulates his pupils. They are exhausted by his restlessness. This drain on their energy will slowly undermine their natural exuberance. In later life it will not be surprising to find them suffering from a lack of zest and vitality.

The teacher who recognizes temperamental imbalance in himself will continually make a conscious effort to overcome his one-sidedness. With children, however, his approach must be less direct. He will have to exercise constant ingenuity and endless patience to achieve his goal. But this goal is identical in both his own and the children's cases; that is, to extend the limits within which their temperaments bind them, to free the self for the attainment of a truly human wholeness.

CHAPTER XI

The Teacher

Has not every teacher worthy of his salt often suspected that he was just as much a problem child as any of his pupils?

At times this feeling can be so depressing as to bring him to the verge of changing his profession. To have experienced such moments may well be proof of a teacher's worthiness. It is a clear indication of his responsible attitude toward the children in his charge. It is a starting point of awareness that can, in a courageous person, lead only to a conscious effort to become more adequate.

In this effort as in all his professional and human striving his fellow teachers in the new art of education will find ways to help him. Every problem that arises for one member of the faculty will be discussed by all in conference. It will be looked upon as a unique opportunity to penetrate more deeply into the riddles of human nature in which all have a common interest.

These conferences will not be infrequent, hurried, perfunctory meetings. They will be the heart through which a school's life blood is continually flowing, the regulator of the whole organism. Here is no principal, no supervisor, no authority to state categorically how a human or teaching problem shall be handled. Every least aspect of the school's total functioning becomes a matter for which every teacher shares joint responsibility. The faculty, rather than some intimidating remote control, even handles such matters as the "hiring and firing" of teachers and the school's finances. Authority for action may be delegated to a member or committee of the faculty, but no action will be taken that has not first been discussed and agreed upon by all.

Such human intercourse has moral value of untold significance. It pervades the school with an atmosphere of unity without which it is hollow at the core. The children will know whether Miss Tompkins and Mr. Jessup and all the others get along together, or whether they are secretly at swords' points. Their cooperation, achieved under the influence of a common faith in human potentiality, will make itself felt as a positive, buoyant spirit upholding teachers and children alike. The achievement of such a spirit will be the first concern of the faculty.

In his intercourse with the children it may seem that the teacher must have achieved almost superhuman stature to be at all adequate. He must have a thorough mastery of subject matter, yet remain naively teachable. He must be as spirited as a race horse, yet gentle, patient, firm in self-control. Even if he has to sit up half the night at a conference or parent-teachers meeting or to prepare his lessons he must be as fresh as a spring morning when he faces his pupils. He must be able to change with lightning swiftness from profundity to wit. He must be a pillar of strength, and at the same time have the fluidic nature of the artist. Is this not requiring the impossible?

But none of these qualities are required to begin with. The teacher enters upon his activity of his own accord. He sets himself the goals that he will follow. If he is really in earnest, it is not long before he undertakes self-transformation.

The creative nature of his task is his strongest ally in acheiving this. His study material is man and universe. How should he remain inadequate when daily he penetrates more deeply into a living knowledge that fills him with enthusiasm

126

and links fragments of learning together into a soul-satisfying unity? He is not called upon to retail an unending succession of sprawling, unrelated facts such as one reads in textbooks. Indeed, he will do well to forget them in the form in which they have been learned. They must then be resurrected in him as living facts, as organic parts of an integrated picture called a "subject."

As he concerns himself with life, with beauty and with wholeness, the teacher begins to be himself more alive, more the artist, more a whole human being. He finds himself developing perceptive faculties of which he never dreamed. As he becomes aware of his growing powers he is filled with a confidence that spurs him forward.

This confidence is not apt to mislead him into self-satisfaction; it is the artist's nature to be forever dissatisfied with what he creates. At the end of each school year he will review his past efforts with the feeling that only now does he know how he should have taught. He will admit that he, not his pupils, has most profited in learning. Realizations such as these fill him with true humility and accelerate his striving.

As he works upon himself the teacher will be increasingly able to lay aside disturbing thoughts and moods brought from his life outside the schoolroom. He must confront his pupils with heart and mind fired with enthusiasm for the material he is about to offer them. As he presents it he will find himself rising above his personal misfortunes, wholly engrossed in the re-creating life of his subject matter.

The living character of this material enables him to do more than teach. It enables him to become a healer—a healer both of his own and his pupils' insufficiencies. He can afford to work slowly with his potent remedies. He is not intent upon a momentary goal; he has a whole lifetime's growth and development in mind. Such an aim makes him as patient as it does untiring.

Often, in his healing efforts, the teacher will be faced with a

127

seemingly insoluble problem in one of his children. In such a case Dr. Steiner recommended that the teacher call up a vivid picture of the child and immerse himself in it before he goes to sleep. On waking he will often discover that his concern has borne fruit in the form of an ingenious idea whereby the problem can readily be solved.

Ingenuity is indeed the very core of the teacher's artistry. He may not possess it as a native talent but his effort itself awakens a creative faculty that grows with exercise. He need not start with superhuman qualities. He need but be intensely interested and unceasingly active, and in time he will no longer be recognizable as the person he was when he began his task.

That he should be continually growing is the least and the most that can be required of him.

CHAPTER XII

Teacher and Child

It was Emerson who said that "to educate a person one must first respect him."

At first we are inclined to agree with this observation. Yet on second thought the word "respect" fails to satisfy us; it suggests a certain remoteness from the learner. Does respect describe our feelings toward the baby whose awkwardness in learning to pronounce our names, to walk, to get a spoonful of food into his mouth without mishap is so enchanting? Do we listen respectfully to the children whom we have taught to paint the drama of a fairy tale in glowing words? Shall the schoolboy, bursting eagerly into the classroom to make us a gift of frog's eggs or to see whether the beans he planted yesterday have sprouted, be welcomed with nothing warmer than respect? Respect is either too small or too large a feeling. It is our hearts that quicken to these experiences.

Yet Emerson was not thinking of this personal side of the teacher-child relationship. He was reminding teachers of the potential grandeur of the human soul, of the eternal image of Man that it is their task to cultivate. We can feel nothing less than reverence for the majesty of this image, so often apparent even in the smallest child.

Not only must the teacher love and reverence his pupils; he must make himself worthy of being reverenced and loved by them. On his ability to do so will depend his real success as an educator. It is not what he knows, but what he *is* that affects the child most deeply, for children instinctively seek in their teacher a model for their own development. If he cannot provide it, their faith in humanity itself is weakened. They become insecure and cannot find their way forward to the full unfolding of their capacities. They are like young vines in their need for strong support.

It may be disturbing to consider how greatly the teacher's qualities influence his pupils. Yet he need not forever remain bogged down in his weaknesses; he can begin at once to overcome them. The very decision to do so will have a beneficial effect upon the children.

It may often happen that when he is feeling most inadequate the children's naive confidence, expressed in a trusting look or an admiring comment, will provide just the tonic needed to restore his flagging spirit.

Such moments illustrate the potency of the relationship possible between teacher and pupils. What he builds into the children is richly returned in a constant interchange. If he believes in them they will reciprocate with their belief in his capacities, continually spurring him on to further effort. His growth in turn will stimulate their growing. It acts dynamically on their unfolding.

Steiner once remarked that to cure a child of an undesirable habit the teacher should not preach to him about it, but instead search out a bad habit in himself and set about its cure. The moral momentum so engendered will have direct effect upon the child.

Teacher and pupils thus continually strive together. There is no question of imposing upon children patterns of behavior foreign to their natures. The teacher who strengthens the human image in himself frees and strengthens his pupils for the gradual building of this image in themselves. They may be far

130

more talented than he—more intelligent, better artists, capable of a stature he may never reach. If so, it need not disturb him. By working to develop his own powers to the utmost he will in the truest sense develop theirs.

*　*　*　*　*　*

Not only must the teacher reverence the children whom he is to educate; he must love them. This will not be difficult. Indeed, he will be constantly amazed at the fact that some kind fate has given such lovable children into his keeping. He sees other teachers with their charges, and gloats in the good fortune that has singled him out to teach the very group he thinks most interesting. They seem to belong to him, and he to them. He feels toward them with all a parent's warmth. Their problems become his problems, their joys his joys. No effort they demand of him will be too great, so keen is his delight at the smallest sign of progress.

The child knows without being told how his teacher feels about him. He can tell it by the welcoming smile and the unhurried handshake given him even when his entrance into the classroom means an interruption of important tasks. He hears it in the pleasant restraint of the teacher's voice greeting him. In the light touch of humor that comes to his rescue in despairing moments he senses how quickly his trouble has been perceived, and how gently remedied. When his naughtiness fails to provoke bursts of anger he knows that it is for his sake that the teacher has controlled himself. Yet when on some rare occasion that usually quiet voice thunders like the wrath of God, he is curiously happy. When the play of lightning around his head is ended, his baser metals have been burned away, and he comes out of his chastening shining gold.

Every class the child attends is a proof of his teacher's devotion. What loving warmth has been spent to make each lesson a gift of life! It pours into the very wording of the teacher's sentences. Here is no dry stuff presented on the pages of a printed course of study. Learning is made an adventure in the land of beauty, a feast of goodness leaving heart, head and limbs rightly nourished. How the floor shakes to the exhilerating rhythms of arithmetic! How small and contracted one feels when the teacher pictures the stunted, strong-rooted plants of the chilly tundra huddling close to the earth! How one expands again at the description of tropical vegetation shooting into giant growth and blossom in the steaming jungle! How noble the form of man becomes as the teacher contrasts it with the animal's! Every learning experience is given a vivid meaning that goes on living and growing with the child's increasing awareness of the world about him.

* * * * * *

When a year of warm companionship and effort has drawn to a close, a kind of harvest festival is celebrated. The schoolroom is decked with the fruits of the whole year's labor. Paintings make the walls bright; forms sculptured in wax or clay and carved in wood are grouped on shelves and tables. The rainbow pages of notebooks lie open, showing maps, diagrams, texts and illustrations. The products of handwork and carpentry fill every available space. There is music of flutes and voices, eurythmy and a play suited to the season.

Before the visitors have arrived for the festivities, teachers and children meet again in their classrooms to look back over all that the year has held in trials and accomplishments. No prizes are given. Instead the teacher speaks briefly about the ways in which every child has made his contribution to the group. Once more the warm pleasure of fellowship is felt—a fellowship in which all have attained new stature.

On parting, the teacher gives each child a letter in lieu of a

132

report on the year's achievements. This is no cold, impersonal, printed piece of pasteboard with a row of marks to fill children with terror or gloating. It is a picture of the child, painted with all the skill of which the teacher is capable. He has taken the greatest pains in composing it. Such a letter is designed to make a deep impression upon the child who receives it, serving both as a milestone of progress and as a stimulus to further effort. If it is artistically rather than pedantically written, the child will absorb its message into the very fibre of his being.

The writing of these letters is a stimulating challenge to the teacher, even though each one may require many struggling hours of effort. He begins by selecting one of his pupils— perhaps six-year-old Susan, whose problems have been much on his mind of late—and conjures up images of this child at work and play. Gestures and expressions characteristic of her nature rise in profusion from the storehouse of his memory. He contemplates them like a portrait painter making a preliminary study of the play of light and feeling in the face of his subject.

As he proceeds with this activity, Susan becomes a vivid presence. He hears the uncanny sweetness of her singing voice and her anger floating shrilly in the window from some recess quarrel. He remembers how flushed her cheecks were that day when measles broke out in the classroom. He sees her fine yellow hair with its electric sparkling, the snapping defiance of her bright blue eyes. He is fascinated by the deftness of her fingers, nimbly guiding the paint-brush in the creation of a quick succession of pictures, or pinching a herd of sheep into lifelike being from a lump of clay. How rapt her eyes are as she listens in complete absorption to a fairy tale! For a moment she has forgotten her feud with the child at the adjoining table.

He sees again the whole-souled reverence with which she knelt before the manger in the Christmas play; her surreptitious cruelty to a puppy that wandered into the schoolyard;

133

the boisterous efficiency embodied in her chunky, vital form; her twinkling feet in red eurythmy slippers; her shy, evasive cunning; her bossy domination over timid schoolmates; her eager response to all real challengers. From each such impression he takes its life and color until the spectrum of her being lies spread out before him, a palette of brightness and shadow.

Now to paint the picture! He dips his brush into the colors and begins.

This is not to be a tinted photograph or a naturalistic portrait to rouse her vanity and stare blankly at her from the canvas. It must rather be a work of art depicting her strengths and weaknesses in symbols. Perhaps he will paint her the picture she can most appreciate: a fairy story.

Taking the colors she has given him he now creates a host of tiny figures. From a pot of rust-red a sly little fox emerges, sharp-nosed and clever-eyed, scarlet tongue lolling as he slips through an enchanted forest carrying a message to the cruel black witch who lives in its dark depths. From a pot of iridescent color comes a fairy with her magic wand in hand, and here's a tiny brave and brawling soldier just back from the wars, sword clanking at his side, equally ready to pick a quarrel or to rescue damsels in distress. In a shining palace high on a hilltop a golden bird sits in a cage and sings to a princess who leans in her window listening. Little does she dream as she leans and listens there what troubles are soon to befall her; how bravely the soldier will fight to save her and to win her hand; how cleverly the fox will do his bit to help; how fairy, golden bird, and all the other actors in the drama will play their parts to make a happy ending.

Susan, each time the story is read to her, lives deeply in its potent imagery. The struggle of good and evil, of beauty and ugliness enacted by the miniature figures, stirs her as preaching never could. She need not recognize it as a picture of her-

134

self, But its effect will be felt as the catharsis of her weaknesses, the enhancement of her strengths for which it was intended.

* * * * * *

In the fifth-grade room another teacher has been wrestling with a different kind of problem. Larry—gray-faced, anemic, skinny—is a ten-year-old newly entered from another school, a confirmed repeater of every grade and almost every possible offense. He is the victim of a drastic reading disability that had gone untreated before the change of school. He is a boy of more than average intelligence, and he feels puzzled and injured at finding himself in the role of dunce and bad boy. He carries a chip on both his stooping shoulders and goes through the world shuffle-footed, stuttering, defeated, attempting to conceal his resentful feelings behind a scowl and an uncertain manner.

From the first he has been treated with quiet friendliness of a kind he has seemingly never known before. Everyone takes an interest in helping him. He begins to thaw a little. He is invited to stay after school several times a week for remedial work and tutoring. Larry agrees in a high-pitched, squeaky voice. But in his gratification at the teacher's interest he leaps the track and tries to draw more attention to himself by putting on a scene. Effort, stupidity, helplessness follow each other in quick succession. Without a word he is quietly dismissed. The next time he makes an appearance his lesson has been learned.

Appropriate curative exercises are administered to remedy his severe digestive sluggishness. Color begins to show in his face and confidence in his bearing. His friendly handshake stiffens. He works well, seldom sulks, and is a pleasant and helpful presence in the classroom.

The letter that his teacher now writes him is not a fairy story. It is a plain, laconic, not in the least patronizing recognition of

135

the great progress he has made—a few philosophic comments on the past campaign from a seasoned soldier to a younger one who has courageously fought his battle and won a first satisfying victory.

*   *   *   *   *   *

The writing of these letters requires real artistry on the teacher's part. Out of each letter his heart and mind must be heard to speak, lovingly, yet not sentimentally; with discernment that has no trace of the negative; voicing encouragement that draws its strength from a recognition of each child's unique potentialities. Every such message becomes a link in the succession of creative acts whereby the child is helped to hew ever closer to his own ideal. It is the potent summing up of the whole year's guidance effort. It is the shining "candle to grow on" of each significant birthday in the school community.

The lot of the teacher who has eight years to spend in the completion of his work with a group of children is an enviable one. Time is a teacher's most important ally. Growth cannot be hurried. The seeds planted in the morning will not have flowered by nightfall. They will require many days and much careful tending for their full unfolding. The teacher who has the element of time to work with will not be bound by hard and fast objectives that force the child's growth to quick conclusion. With eight years at his disposal he can afford to become a long-term planner, meeting the needs of the moment flexibly. His teaching will therefore be as organic as the children's own development.

Yet each step in learning has been carefully prepared. Long before the time is ripe for a new phase of instruction the teacher will have made the soil ready for the planting.

He will not need to test the children's knowledge at the beginning of each new school year. He knows their capacities

136

intimately from past performance, and he is not intent upon knowledge for its own sake. Acquiring knowledge is only part of a child's whole growth—growth beyond evaluation by any paper test.

In the eight-year span allotted to them, teacher and pupils can breathe freely and unhurriedly. An immense warmth springs up between them in this easy atmosphere. They become a closely knit group. Yet their work together under the teacher's inspiring leadership holds them to the highest level of human intercourse. There is none of the degrading familiarity that can so easily destroy the dignity of group relations. It does not occur to the children to call the teacher in whom wisdom and strength are personified, "Nick" or "Johnny." He is a beloved authority to whom all look up with deepest reverence.

The teacher on his part will never be satisfied with himself nor with his teaching. He will continually strive to become a more worthy representative of humanity, a finer artist, a keener student of man and nature. Yet, says Rudolf Steiner, he will have succeeded in his efforts if he has been able to call forth in children during the first phase of their development the feeling "the world is good"; in the second "the world is beautiful"; in the third "the world is true."

BIBLIOGRAPHY

1. Books by Rudolf Steiner

Balance in Teaching. 2nd ed. Spring Valley, NY: Mercury Press, 1982. 58 pages.

Deeper Insights in Education: The Waldorf Approach. Trans. René Querido. Spring Valley, NY: Anthroposophic Press, 1983. 63 pages.

Discussions with Teachers. Trans. Helen Fox. London: Rudolf Steiner Press, 1967. 168 pages.

Education as a Social Problem. Trans. Lisa D. Monges and Doris M. Bugbey. Spring Valley, NY: Anthroposophic Press, 1969. 115 pages.

Education as an Art. Ed. Paul M. Allen. Trans. Michael Tapp and Elisabeth Tapp. Blauvelt, NY: Steinerbooks, Garber Communications, 1970. 126 pages.

The Education of the Child in the Light of Anthroposophy. Trans. Mary Adams and George Adams. 2nd ed. London: Rudolf Steiner Press, 1975.

Essentials of Education. Trans. Jesse Darrell. 2nd ed. London: Rudolf Steiner Press, 1968. 95 pages.

The Four Temperaments. Trans. Frances E. Dawson. 2nd ed. Spring Valley, NY: Anthroposophic Press, 1976. 59 pages.

Human Values in Education. Trans. Vera Compton-Burnett. London: Rudolf Steiner Press, 1971. 190 pages.

The Kingdom of Childhood. Trans. Helen Fox. London: Rudolf Steiner Press, 1964. 165 pages.

Lectures to Teachers. Trans. Daphne Harwood. 2nd ed. London: Anthroposophical Publishing Company, 1931. 95 pages.

A Modern Art of Education. Trans. Jesse Darrell and George Adams. 3rd ed. London: Rudolf Steiner Press, 1954. 232 pages.

Practical Advice to Teachers. Trans. Johanna Collis. 2nd ed. London: Rudolf Steiner Press, 1976. 206 pages.

Prayers for Mothers and Children. Trans. Eileen V. Hersey and Christian von Arnim. 3rd ed. London: Rudolf Steiner Press, 1983. 78 pages.

The Renewal of Education through the Science of the Spirit. Trans. Roland Everett. Bournemouth. England: Kolisko Archive, for Steiner Schools Fellowship, 1981. 217 pages.

The Roots of Education. Trans. Helen Fox. London: Rudolf Steiner Press, 1968. 95 pages.

A Social Basis for Primary and Secondary Education. Forest Row, England: Michael Hall School, 1958, mimeographed. 43 pages.

The Spiritual Ground of Education. Trans. Daphne Harwood. London: Anthroposophical Publishing Company, 1947. 136 pages.

Study of Man: General Education Course. Trans. A. C. Harwood. 2nd ed. London: Rudolf Steiner Press, 1966. 191 pages.

Three Lectures for Teachers. Forest Row, England: Steiner Schools Fellowship, n.d., mimeographed. 25 pages.

Waldorf Education for Adolescence. Bournemouth, England: Kolisko Archive, for Steiner Schools Fellowship, 1980. 107 pages.

2. *General Treatments by Other Authors*

Aeppli, Willi. *The Care and Development of the Human Senses.* Trans. Valerie Freilich. Forest Row, England: Steiner Schools Fellowship, n.d. 84 pages.

Baravalle, Hermann von. *The International Waldorf School Movement.* Spring Valley, NY: Waldorf School Monographs, St. George Book Service, 1960. 50 pages.

Carlgren, Frans. *Education towards Freedom.* Ed. Joan Rudel and Siegfried Rudel. East Grinstead, England: Lanthorn Press, 1981. 208 pages.

Easton, Stewart C. "The New Art of Education. The Waldorf School Movement" in *Man and World in the Light of Anthroposophy.* 2nd ed. Spring Valley, NY: Anthroposophic Press, 1982. Pp. 382–411.

Edmunds, Francis. Rudolf Steiner Education: The Waldorf Schools. London: Rudolf Steiner Press, 1979. 134 pages.

Harwood, A. C(ecil). *The Recovery of Man in Childhood: A Study in the Educational Work of Rudolf Steiner.* Spring Valley, NY: Anthroposophic Press, 1981 1958. 208 pages.

————, *The Way of a Child: An Introduction to the Work of Rudolf Steiner for Children.* London: Rudolf Steiner Press, 1967. 144 pages.

Heydebrand, Caroline von, comp. *The Curriculum of the First Waldorf School.* Ed. with additions Eileen Hutchins. Forest Row, England: Steiner Schools Fellowship, 1966. 75 pages.

Holtzapfel, Walter. *Children's Destinies: The Three Directions of Man's Development.* Trans. Madge Childs. 2nd ed. Spring Valley, NY: Mercury Press, 1984. 90 pages.

Howard, Alan. *You Wanted to Know . . . What a Waldorf School Is . . . And What It Is Not.* Spring Valley, NY: St. George Publications, 1983. 53 pages.

Jarman, Ron, ed. *Child and Man Extracts.* Forest Row, England: Steiner Schools Fellowship, 1975. 435 pages.

Lissau, Magda. *The Temperaments and the Arts: Their Relation and Function in Waldorf Pedagogy*. Chicago: Magda Lissau, 1983; Distributed by St. George Book Service, Spring Valley, NY. 135 pages.

Lyons, Nick and Piening, Ekkehard, eds. *Educating as an Art: Essays on the Rudolf Steiner Method—Waldorf Education*. New York: Rudolf Steiner School Press, 1979; Distributed by Anthroposophic Press, Spring Valley, NY. 183 pages.

Querido, René. *Creativity in Education*. San Francisco: Dakin, 1982. 77 pages.

Richards, M(ary). C(aroline). *Toward Wholeness: Rudolf Steiner Education in America*. Middletown, CT: Wesleyan University Press, 1980. 210 pages.

Rist, Georg and Schneider, Peter. *Integrating Vocational and General Education: A Rudolf Steiner School*. Hamburg, West Germany: UNESCO Institute for Education, 1979; Distributed by unipub, Ann Arbor, MI. 196 pages.

Stockmeyer, E. A. Karl. *Rudolf Steiner's Curriculum for Waldorf Schools*. Trans. R. Everett-Zade. Forest Row: Steiner Schools Fellowship, 1982. 240 pages.

Wilkinson, Roy. *Commonsense Schooling*. East Grinstead, England: Henry Goulden, 1978. 98 pages.

————. *The Curriculum of the Rudolf Steiner School*. Forest Row, England: Roy Wilkinson, 1982. 29 pages.

————. *Questions and Answers on Rudolf Steiner Education*. East Grinstead, England: Henry Goulden, 1980. 33 pages.

3. On Specific Subjects by Other Authors

Baravalle, Hermann von. *Astronomy: An Introduction*. Spring Valley, NY: Waldorf School Monographs, St. George Book Service, 1974. 40 pages.

————. *Geometric Drawing and the Waldorf School Plan*. Spring Valley, NY: Waldorf School Monographs, St. George Book Service, 1967. 56 pages.

————. *Introduction to Physics in the Waldorf Schools*. Spring Valley, NY: Waldorf School Monographs, St. George Book Service, 1962. 41 pages.

————. *Perspective Drawing*. Spring Valley, NY: Waldorf School Monographs, St. George Book Service, 1960. 46 pages.

————. *The Teaching of Arithmetic and the Waldorf School Plan*. Spring Valley, NY: Waldorf School Monographs, St. George Book Service, 1967. 40 pages.

Frohlich, Margaret and Niederhauser, Hans. *Form Drawing*. Spring Valley, NY: Mercury Press, 1984. 57 pages.

Gabert, Erich. *Punishment in Self-Education and in the Education of the Child*. Trans. Pauline Wehrle. Forest Row, England: Steiner Schools in Fellowship, n.d. 52 pages.

Glas, Werner. *The Waldorf School Approach to History*. Spring Valley, NY: Anthroposophic Press, 1981. 102 pages.

Gorge, Alice A. *Creative Toymaking*. 2nd ed. Edinburgh, Great Britain: Floris Books, 1981. 58 pages.

Grahl, Ursula. *The Wisdom in Fairy Tales*. East Grinstead, England: New Knowledge Books, 1969. 43 pages.

Hahn, Herbert. *From the Wellsprings of the Soul: Towards the Religious Teaching of the Young*. Trans. Anne Barnes. Forest Row: Steiner Schools Fellowship, 1977. 107 pages.

Hauck, Hedwig. *Handwork and Handicrafts from Indications by Rudolf Steiner, Part 1*. Trans. Graham Rickett. Forest Row, England: Steiner Schools Fellowship, 1968. 101 pages.

Jaffke, Freya. *Making Soft Toys*. Trans. Rosemary Gebert. Edinburgh, Great Britain: Floris Books, 1981. 59 pages.

Kolisko, Eugen. *Elementary Chemistry: Combustion, Lime, Salt, Water, Metals*. Bournemouth, England: Kolisko Archive, 1978. 30 pages.

————. *Geology*. Bournemouth, England: Kolisko Archives, 1979. 18 pages.

————. *Natural History*. Bournemouth, England: Kolisko Archive, 1979. 22 pages.

McAllen, Audrey. *Teaching Children to Write: Its Connection with the Development of Spatial Consciousness*. London: Rudolf Steiner Press, 1977. 80 pages.

————. *The Extra Lesson: Exercises in Movement, Drawing and Painting for Helping Children in Difficulties with Writing, Reading and Arithmetic*. London: Audrey McAllen, 1974. 78 pages.

Strauss, Michaela. *Understanding Children's Drawings*. London: Rudolf Steiner Press, 1978. 95 pages.

Wilkinson, Roy, A series of numerous booklets on teaching many individual subjects, such as *Teaching History* (4 vols.), *Teaching Mathematics, Teaching English, Teaching Geography, The Interpretation of Fairy Tales*, etc.) Forest Row, England: Roy Wilkinson.

4. For Parents

Carey, Diana and Large, Judy. *Festivals, Family and Food.* Stroud, England: Hawthorne Press, 1982. 223 pages.

Cusick, Lois. *Waldorf Parenting Handbook: Useful Information on Child Development and Education from Anthroposophical Sources.* 2nd ed. Spring Valley, NY: St. George Publications, 1984. 160 pages.

Glas, Norbert. *Conception, Birth and Early Childhood.* Spring Valley, NY: Anthroposophic Press, 1983. 154 pages.

Davy, Gudrun and Voors, Bons, eds. *Lifeways: Working with Family Questions.* Stroud, England: Hawthorne Press, 1983. 216 pages.

König, Karl. *Brothers and Sisters: The Order of Birth in the Family.* Spring Valley, NY: Anthroposophic Press and Edinburgh, Great Britain: Floris Books, 1984. 91 pages.

_____. *The First Three Years of the Child.* Spring Valley, NY: Anthroposophic Press and Edinburgh, Great Britain: Floris Books, 1983. 136 pages.

Large, Martin. *Who's Bringing Them Up? Television and Child Development.* Stroud, England: Hawthorne Press, 1980. 136 pages.

Linden, Wilhelm zur. *A Child Is Born: Pregnancy, Birth, Early Childhood.* London: Rudolf Steiner Press, 1980. 223 pages.

Sleigh, Julian. *Thirteen to Nineteen: Growing Free.* Edinburgh, Great Britain: Floris Books, 1982. 32 pages.

Smith, Susan. *Echoes of a Dream: Creative Beginnings for Parent and Child.* London, Canada: Waldorf School Association of London, 1982. 68 pages.